Mary Virginia

March 1710

Reaching for God

Reaching for God

Eileen Mitson

CHRISTIAN HERALD BOOKS
Chappaqua, New York

Reaching For God

Life eternal is nought other than that blessed
regard wherewith Thou never ceasest to behold me;
yea, even the secret places of my soul.
With Thee, to behold is to give life;
'tis unceasingly to impart sweetest love of Thee;
'tis to inflame me to love of Thee by love's imparting,
and to feed me by inflaming,
and by feeding to kindle my yearning,
and by kindling to make me drink of the dew of gladness,
and by drinking to infuse in me a fountain of life,
and by infusing to make it increase and endure.

Nicholas of Cusa.
THE VISION OF GOD

Grateful acknowledgment is made for permission to
quote from the following:

The Vision of God by Nicholas of Cusa published by
Frederick Ungar Publishing Co.

Pursuit of God by A. W. Tozer published by Christian
Publications, Inc.

The Problem of Pain by C. S. Lewis published by
Macmillan Publishing Co., Inc.

Spirits in Bondage by C. S. Lewis published by
Macmillan Publishing Co., Inc.

The Silver Chair by C. S. Lewis published by Macmillan
Publishing Co., Inc.

Hound of Heaven by Francis Thompson published by
Peter Pauper Press

Four Quartets by T. S. Eliot published by Harcourt Brace
Jovanovich

Foreword

I make no apology for the fact that the epigraph to this book is taken from the writings of a saint who lived four hundred years ago. One of our best loved evangelical writers also had a high regard for Nicholas of Cusa, so I feel that I am in good company. A.W. Tozer, in his book *Pursuit of God* writes:

I should like to say more about this old man of God. He is not much known today anywhere among Christian believers, and among current fundamentalists he is known not at all. I feel that we could gain much from a little acquaintance with men of his spiritual flavor, and the school of Christian thought which they represent. Christian literature, to be accepted and approved by the evangelical leaders of our times, must follow very closely the same train of thought, a kind of "party line" from which it is scarcely safe to depart. A half century of this has made us smug and content. We imitate each other with slavish devotion, and our most strenuous efforts are put forth to try to say the same thing that everyone around is saying—and yet to find an excuse for saying it, some little safe variation on the approved theme, or, if no more, at least a new illustration.

9

Nicholas was a true follower of Christ, a lover of the Lord, radiant and shining in his devotion to the person of Jesus. His theology was orthodox, but fragrant and sweet, as everything about Jesus might be properly expected to be. His conception of eternal life, for instance, is beautiful in itself, and, if I mistake not, is nearer in spirit to John 17:3 than that which is current among us today.

Nicholas' conception of eternal life, as expressed in my epigraph, is really the theme of this book. Readers who are looking for another "Holy Spirit" book will be disappointed, although there may be points in my narrative which seem to be heading in that direction. Nor have I followed very closely the "party line" of which Tozer speaks so aptly. I share very much his feelings about the kind of Christian literature which needs to conform to a certain pattern in order to be accepted and approved by the evangelical leaders of our time. Nor is this book simply a safe variation on the approved theme.

It is rather a simple and I hope honest account of one woman's experience of God in her life. The experience will not fit into any standard pattern, any more than the author as an individual, can be made to fit into any particular mould. I have simply told how God, in his infinite mercy and grace, has chosen to reveal himself to me; how he has made me to "drink of the dew of gladness, and by drinking, to infuse in me a fountain of life."

Eileen Mitson

Part One

All your life an unattainable ecstasy has hovered just
beyond the grasp of your consciousness. The day is
coming when you will wake to find, beyond all hope,
that you have attained it, or else that it was within
your reach and you have lost it forever.

C.S. Lewis
THE PROBLEM OF PAIN

1

THERE WAS A SPRING in the meadow at the back of the
farmhouse where I was born and spent my childhood.
An iron pump, enclosed by wooden railings and accessi-
ble by means of a small, rickety gate, drew the cold
spring water up out of the bowels of the earth to supply
our household with all its requirements for drinking,
washing and cooking. As far as I remember, my father,
or one of the farm hands, fetched this water every day in
heavy zinc buckets and deposited them on the bricked
floor of the kitchen, and after that it was up to my mother
to make it go as far as possible. The pump was a few
minutes walk from the house, and on rare occasions my
sister and I were sent to fetch a bucketful of water when
supplies in the house were running low. We set off, each
holding one side of the handle, and chanting to each
other as we went: "Jack and Jill went up the hill-To fetch a
pail of water...."

From the back of the farmhouse, across a cobbled back
yard, round an outhouse where beer had been brewed
many years ago, and where there was still an old brick
oven once used for baking bread, along a grass path

13

which led into the first meadow we would go, stopping
to admire the profusion of pink "plum-pudding" flowers
which filled a dried-up pond just inside the meadow.
Then around a second pond where minnows darted in
the brown, muddy water, through an open five-barred
gate and into the long meadow where the pump stood.

When we had let ourselves into the small enclosure,
my sister who was one year older than me, and was
consequently expected to take the main burden of re-
sponsibility in these matters, took from the bottom of the
bucket an enamel jug of water which had been saved by
my mother from the previous supply, and lifting a kind
of iron lid on the top of the pump, handed me the jug and
said:

"When I say *Now!*"

She then took the long, curved handle of the pump in
her two hands and lifted it high above her head. (We
couldn't have been more than about seven and eight at
the time, because civilization spread its arms out to reach
us shortly before the beginning of World War II, and two
gleaming brass taps magically appeared over the stone
sink in the kitchen, making the pump extraneous.)
"Now:" my sister commanded, and I, straining on
tip-toe with my jug of water poised at the ready, tipped it
into the long, thirsty neck of the rusty pump. Immediately, Sylvia pumped the handle furiously up and down;
and sure enough, with a gurgle and a splutter, the mouth
of the pump belched forth yard after yard of clear, sparkling water into the waiting bucket. I once asked my
father why the pump would not give forth of its bounty
until that jugful of water left over from a previous supply
had been offered to it. I forget the answer now, though
no doubt the more scientifically minded would be able to
give the reason right away. Yet the principle upon which

the pump worked has somehow remained in my mind over the years as an analogy of a spiritual truth: not until we are prepared to offer up that small, hard-won jugful of human achievement, that pitifully precious supply of self-esteem which we guard so jealously, can the limitless waters of eternal life be released in us. But once we have upended the little tin jug and cast ourselves down at the life-giving mouth of the spring, then we know, without doubt, that it is the water for which we have always, thirsted. It is the very source of joy. It is the spring of life, clear as crystal, proceeding out of the throne of God.

When, in my late teens, I discovered the writings of C. S. Lewis, I began to see for the first time that much of our human experience, especially the vivid, richly felt experiences of childhood, has at the core this quest for eternal life. "If I find in myself a desire which no experience in this world can satisfy," says Lewis, "then the most probable explanation is that I was made for another world." The simplicity of this logic still strikes me like a beam of pure truth each time I read it. It is the answer to man's spiritual thirst, the reason for the deep, unspoken need that lies hidden in each of us.

Our farmhouse was in the very heart of the country. It was a long, gray house with twin gables, and the front door was slightly off-center. To one side of the door were two large reception rooms, and to the left a long, spacious lounge, or sitting room as we then called it. A long corridor led from this room along the length of the house to a side door, which was the entry we used most of the time. As you entered this door, the kitchen lay to your right, the dining room to the left, and the long corridor stretched ahead of you to the big room at the end of the house. Between the dining room and the lounge was a room which changed its identity several times during the twenty years I lived there. During the war it became a bedroom for the whole family, while the upstairs was inhabited by evacuees. But in pre-war days it was used as a small sitting room, because the large lounge, together with the room above it, was let out to 'London folk' who came down for several weeks during the summer, and at odd week-ends the rest of the year.

When the 'middle' room was a sitting room, a huge sideboard complete with mirror, stood opposite the window. The window looked out over the front lawn, and beyond to the farmyard. The granary, the stables, cowsheds, and barn were all visible from here, as well as a large pond surrounded by evergreens, and a huge cherry tree which stood at the bottom of the lawn, and was a mass of snowy white blossom in spring. Between the farm building and the pond, a long, rough drive led up to a narrow road at the top. The road led to the village in one direction, and to the woods in the other. From three sides of the house, no other sign of human habitation appeared—not even a distant chimney. Only corn fields and pastures and woodland. On the fourth side, my grandfather's redbrick farmhouse was just visible across the fields.

One of my earliest memories is that of climbing on to the back of the sofa in the "middle" room, and from there on to the sideboard, to peer into the mirror. It was not my own image that I wanted to see, but the image of a magic world which, as I bounced up and down on the sofa, offered me tantalizing glimpses of itself in the mirror. Now, as I crouched on the sideboard, that magic world was only inches away. For there was the whole farmyard scene, so well-loved, so familiar, reflected for me in the sideboard's gleaming mirror. There were the barns, the stables and the cherry tree, but on the wrong side of

the yard. And there was the pond, dark, green and mysterious, on my left instead of my right, while beyond it lay
meadows I had never run in, and trees I had never sat
under. Furthermore, the whole scene lay spread out, not
at the front of the house, but at the back, where the
kitchen garden should be. From where I knelt, I should
have been looking out at the northern sky; instead, gold-
en sunlight streamed at me from out of the southern sky.

In that moment, lasting perhaps only seconds, or at
the most minutes, I was in the land of Never-Never. I
would not have been surprised to find it peopled by the
characters from the fairy-story books I loved so much;
Jack, who climbed the beanstalk to a world above the
clouds, or the golden-haired girl who fell down a well
while trying to retrieve her ball, only to find herself in a
land of indescribable beauty far, far below.

Some of the illustrations from those books are etched
indelibly on my mind. The blue-green palace of the
Snow Queen, with its towers and turrets stretching upward into icy infinity; the enchanted woods and forests
where hidden dangers lay in wait for the unwary; the
noble-browed princes on powerful white steeds, and the
lovely princesses with their melancholy-sweet faces;
their milk-white skin, pale violet eyes and hair like spun
gold or black as a raven's wing. I reached out with unconscious longing toward the rainbow's end, to the secrets
that lay at the back of the North Wind, to the back-to-
front world spread out before me now in the sideboard
mirror. What if my hand did touch only cold, inpenetra-
ble glass? The longing itself, though unconscious, was
real enough, and was to become more so with the passing years.

"But these things," C. S. Lewis reminded us in one of
his broadcast talks, "these things—the beauty, the

memory of our own past—are good images of what we
really desire; but if they are mistaken for the thing itself,
they turn into dumb idols, breaking the hearts of their
worshippers. For they are not the thing itself; they are
only the scent of a flower we have not found, the echo of
a tune we have not heard, news from a country we have
never yet visited. . . ."

Is this thirst, this longing, common to us all, and do we
all feel it with equal intensity? Or do we differ only in the
degree with which we are willing to recognize and to
savour the need? I have never been sure. But in the same
address from which I have just quoted, C. S. Lewis says
something which I have found to be true in my own
experience as a communicator. He says:

"In speaking of this desire for our own far-off country,
which we find in ourselves even now, I feel a certain
shyness. I am almost committing an indecency. I am
trying to rip open the inconsolable secret in each of
you. . . ."

Once, when trying to speak of these things to a large
gathering of people, I was overcome by the same sense of
restraint, an embarrassment not unlike that of finding
oneself observed in an intimate embrace.

Can it be that we have become so bound hand and foot
by the graveclothes of materialism and superficial values
that we have become strangers to the real, the spiritual,
the transcendant meaning of life? It is a sobering thought.

2

BUT HANS CHRISTIAN ANDERSEN and the brothers Grimm were not the only sources from which my childish imagination was fed. My sister and I must have had at least as many Bible story books as fairy tales upon our shelves. Again, the illustrations in some of these are as clearly etched upon my mind as if I saw them only yesterday. Elijah by the brook Cedron being fed by ravens; Abraham about to sacrifice his child Isaac; young Samuel in the Temple raising himself on one elbow in the murky-purple gloom of the ancient building to listen again for the compelling voice of the Lord . . . and even if the sheets on little Samuel's bed did look a bit too much like the ones my mother stirred around in the brick copper in the corner of our kitchen with her long, wooden, heat-bleached pole on wash day; and if the bread the ravens fed to Elijah did look more like flat stones from the brook itself, yet the majesty and wonder of it all was no less powerful. I gazed and gazed at the beautiful, breathtaking spectacle of Elijah being taken up to heaven in a chariot of fire, only stopping to wonder briefly why the chariot needed wheels; and I lingered with delicious horror over the prostrate Isaac, with the point of the deadly looking dagger only inches away from his innocent breast. But then, there was the captive ram with his strong, curled horns caught in the cruel thicket, and SALVATION might just as well have been written in letters of burning gold in the lowering sky beyond the dreadful scene.

The preacher explained from the pulpit of the little chapel overlooking the village green that I was looking at a timeless event: at the lamb slain before the foundation of the world, a substitutionary sacrifice for lost mankind. His words may have seemed dry and meaningless to my childish mind; but the truth behind them was already there, a dormant seedling in the darkness of my unconscious.

We went, my sister and I, three times every Sunday to chapel. In the morning and evening we went with our parents, taking the narrow road that led from the top of our drive to the village green. In the afternoon we ran across the meadows that separated us from our grandfather's house, through his farmyard which opened straight out on to the green itself. The chapel and the village school, both red brick buildings of similiar size, smiled benignly from the other side of the green. Clustered around the green, which was cut in half by the road to the village itself, were several thatched cottages and a small tiled house which was the home of the resident minister of the chapel.

For us children, a special aura hovered about anyone who had not actually been born and bred in the village. The minister and his wife came under this category, and we viewed them with a certain amount of awe and wonder. The minister preached two good evangelical sermons every Sunday, and I don't remember ever being really bored. There was so much to see, to smell, to hear, to touch. The thick, varnished pew had a special feel under my exploring hands; the hymn books smelled fusty from years of contact with the cold, damp interior of the vestry cupboard, and the old "slow-but-sure" Tortoise stove filled the chapel with its acrid, pungent warmth in winter.

My father always took a small bag of extra strong mints to chapel in his pocket. At the beginning of the sermon, to the embarrassment of my mother, but not, until we were much older, to us, he would push his large, work-hardened hand into the bag, and after what seemed to us like an endless time of rustling, produce a mint and pass it along to my sister at the far end of the row via my mother and me. Then back went his hand into the bag again, rustle, rustle, rustle, and after a while a second mint appeared, to be passed across my mother directly to me. Then one for mother, which she sometimes refused, sometimes took impatiently, willing him to stop the now almost deafening rustling and settle back for the sermon; which, after his own "pepnit" as he pronounced it, had been popped into his mouth, he eventually did. And so while our pew must have been sending up clouds of mint-scented air to waft tantalizingly, or otherwise, across the nostrils of other worshipers, the great Bible truths would be uttered from the pulpit. And we would sit there, our ears still tingling from the gusto of our own hearty singing, our hearts aglow with the friendly famil-iarity of the great rolling phrases that came from the preacher's lips, and our throats burning from the impact of the mints which, I decided anew each Sunday of my young life, were really too strong for me anyway.

Nearly everybody in the congregation was a relative of mine. There was an uncle who always stood with his

right arm lifted in a backwards position from the side of
his body, as if to ward off some hidden danger lurking
behind him while he sang. My mother, who was always
ready for a good giggle (though never, may it be said, in
chapel) would give me a nudge and a nod in Uncle
Herby's direction on the days when the arm seemed to be
held extra wide of his short, hunched body. Our cousin
Daphne was several years older than us and wore neat,
fashionable clothes and trim, bow-decorated court
shoes. We envied her that extra measure of sophistica-
tion the added years gave her, but loved her because she
treated us as equals. I remember one Sunday when she
bent over me to give me an affectionate squeeze, telling
her that she smelled of strawberry jam. It was the highest
compliment I could think of. Another girl of fifteen or so
might have been highly indignant, but not so Daphne. I
can still hear her peal of delighted laughter as she told me
it must be the vanishing cream she wore under her face
powder. I secretly longed for the day when I would smell
like strawberry jam too.

I was going to say that we girls never saw the inside of
a cinema until we were in our teens, but that would not
be quite true. We must have been quite young when we
were taken one day by our parents into the local market
town eight miles away to see a film of the recent coronation of George V. I remember nothing about the cinema,
or the coronation, but recollect clearly the nature of our
departure from the building. The film of the coronation
must have been over, and the "Big Film" just beginning,
because I remember feeling tension building up in my
mother as she sat beside me in the semi-darkness. Upon
the screen a beautiful woman appeared, her hair immac-
ulately waved, her wide mouth smiling. Then a handsome man, like no one I'd ever seen in the vicinity of the

village green. Suddenly there appeared on the screen the close-up of some kind of number chart. Was it a gambling board, or just a calendar? At any rate, a large forefinger was the next to appear, and it began to point to the numbers one by one. As it rested on a number, the face of the smiling girl would appear, and she would shake her head roguishly. 27? 22? 25? the silent, moving finger enquired. And each time the girl shook her well-groomed head. Then the finger came to rest on 24, and the girl's head nodded, still wearing that roguish smile. Puzzled, I continued to watch the magic screen, but just at that moment my father whispered something to my mother, she in turn bent toward us children and said in a low voice:

"We're leaving now."

"But why, mum, why?"

"Jesus wouldn't like it if we stayed."

Quietly the four of us got up and tiptoed out of the cinema. When I asked my mother later about the pointing finger, she said she supposed the man was guessing the woman's age. I shrugged, and never gave the matter another thought.

3

MY MOTHER was the center, the refuge, the life-giving heartbeat of my childhood. It was to her that I turned for all my needs. Her body's warmth, the touch and the smell of her, the sound of her voice, her infectious laughter became a part of the texture of my life. I would climb onto her lap as she sat at the kitchen table after a meal and wind my arms around her neck, burying my face in the soft warmth beneath her chin.

"Get off my neck! My collar cost me ninepence!" she would cry. But she went on cuddling and tickling and laughing and covering me with kisses. It was all part of the ritual. My sister would join in, attacking my mother from behind, but being of a rather less demonstrative nature, she would wait for me to initiate the procedure. Often in the summer, in the middle of one of these romps, my mother would say:

"Let's leave the washing up and go and sit in the meadow!"

And up we would all leap, leaving the table littered with remains of rabbit pie, rice pudding and stewed plums; we would grab a heavy red leather overcoat from the passage—a once-gorgeous garment bequeathed to us by the wealthy "London folk" who rented our west wing—and make for the back door. Round the brew-house (pronounced "brewuss" by all of us, but later christened, more genteely, the "woodshed") we dashed, through the gate into the meadow, and there in the sunniest, grassiest spot we could find we would spread out the leather coat with its grubby white furry lining uppermost, and hurl ourselves down on our backs. My mother and I soaked up the sun like cats. We could never have enough of it. But again I seem to remember that Sylvia could not stand too much heat, and often wandered off into the shade. We were both blonde, but her skin had that extra fairness which reacts to strong sunlight. Her hair was a lovely silver-blonde, while mine was more gold in tone. Whether it is that memory is basically a self-centered recording instrument, I'm not sure, but at any rate many of my memories of this time in my life seem to involve scenes in which my mother and I feature together, with Sylvia a shadowy figure on the periphery. Possibly this trick of memory is a result of the deep emotional need that I had for my mother at this time.

My mother was my friend, my comforter, my instructor, my guide, and my ally against the explosive temper of my father. This would not be a true picture of my childhood, or a true account of a spiritual journey, if I did not mention at the outset that my early days were colored by this trait in my father which spoilt an otherwise warm and affectionate nature. The slightest thing would rouse him into a raging temper which made the veins stand out in his face, his blue eyes flash, and his wide mouth bellow forth threats which made us children curl up in terror. He tended to show favoritism toward me, as the youngest child, although before my birth he very much hoped I would be a boy. He called me "Dick" for a number of years, and when I showed unusual promise at school, proudly boasted of my prowess to anyone who would care to listen.

But he never knew how much I feared and dreaded his fits of rage. In spite of his obvious affection for me, the whole fabric of our father-daughter relationship was, for me, undermined and invalidated by the violence of his temper. This was rarely aimed directly at me, but at us two little girls together. He would shout and rave at us, threatening us with violent punishment over the most trivial thing. By the time I was four, I had developed a bad stammer which was to affect me for years to come, leaving me with a paralysing fear of having to open my mouth in public. When I could not curl up on my mother's lap, I curled up within myself, shrinking in terror from any situation which might bring down my father's wrath.

To make matters worse, his irascible nature had given him a bad reputation in the village. The fact that we were all stalwarts of the local chapel only made matters worse. At school, the other children teased us about our father, referring to him as "portable Ernie"—a phrase which puzzles me to this day, since I have rarely heard the word "portable" used to convey any other meaning than that of a movable object. My father was certainly movable, in the emotional realm, if not in the physical, but that is not what they meant! But we knew what they did mean, and were deeply, angrily ashamed. That our father, to whom we would have liked to give the respect which by nature we knew was due to a father, should be spoken of with such contemptuous disrespect by the children of other farm workers and laborers was unbearable. To make matters worse, we had nothing to say in his defense, though we tried, verbally, to hit back at the jeerers.

Possibly a less sensitive child than I would have shrugged off these things, or somehow made herself immune, but for me there was no escape. My secret misery over the situation grew with the years, and it was not until I was in my early teens that I was able to come to terms with it. I remember a day which seems, as I look back, to have marked a turning point in my relationship with my father.

He had taught me, when I was about twelve, to drive a tractor, so that I could help with the harvest during school holidays. I loved this outdoor life, and spent many golden days out in the fields, doing a shuttle service between field and stackyard with trailers of corn. I enjoyed the company of the farm workers immensely, and I think they enjoyed mine. Their rough good humor, and their friendliness, their simple country philosophy and their love of the land forged a bond between us which I prized. I found that I was able to give to them the kind of respect which I longed to be able to give my father.

Then one day when we were all laughing hilariously in the field over something which had gone wrong—I cannot recall what it was, but it was something which delayed my return to the haystack with my load of corn— my father came raging down the field and berated the men in his loud, bellowing voice for their incompetence. The men stood quietly by while he raged on, saying nothing, but looking at him with thinly-veiled scorn. I looked from the mild-mannered men to my raging father, and something in me snapped. I picked up my coat and strode off over the fields for home. Part of me was expecting him to yell after me, while another part of me knew with calm assurance that he would do nothing of the kind. No mention of the incident was made when he came in for dinner, though he must have had to take over the tractor-driving himself after I had left the field. But from that day I was no longer afraid of him.

I must have known before that incident that his bark was worse than his bite, but the point is that it was not his bite that damaged me. Despite all the colorful threats he leveled against us children when we were young, I cannot remember that he ever struck either of us. But I know now that verbal violence can be more destructive, and is probably more psychologically harmful, than actual physical violence. I am not here attempting to apportion blame, but simply to state the facts as I remember them. We are none of us immune from blame for damage we may have done to others, especially we who are parents, through faults of which we may have been totally unaware at the time. Humankind is caught up in a web of cause and effect, in a complex pattern of behavior and heredity; often we are trapped between tides over which we have only partial control.

And I ask myself, may not the person that I now am, the urge to creativity which I find within myself, at least owe as much to my neurotic fear of my father, as to the mother whom I loved so deeply, or to my paternal grandmother from whom I am said to inherit my poetic tendencies? And how can I tell what spiritual conflicts went on behind those purple rages, or what hidden depths in my father's nature might not have given birth to the essence which is me? The grace of God works through what is base as well as through what is good, else were we all without hope. We are all infected by the original sin of our first parents in Eden; and we pass on the blight, in one way or another, to our children. There were times when I became inordinately angry with my own children, and saw their frightened faces cowering from my violent words. And I ask myself, what did they see that brought such fear to their eyes? Did they see the same image of rage that I once saw in my own father? Was the same demon reproduced, in a measure, in me? And if so, what harm, what further damage may I not have done? There is none righteous, no not one. And let him that is without sin cast the first stone.

One picture of my father stands out in my mind with vivid clarity. In the shed at the side of the house, he is beating our black retriever, Rover. Rover's crime? He has run away. The evidence? A broken chain. Though Rover has obviously returned after his brief spree, yet he must be punished.

My mother hears the sounds from the shed and rushes out to intervene. "Stop, stop!" she cries, almost beside herself with anguish and indignation: Rover has not strayed. The link in the chain snapped earlier that day whilst Rover was barking at a tradesman. Rover himself has not moved from the shed all day. My father stands there with the stick in his hand. His eyes blur over with remorse. Shamefacedly he looks down at the dumb, cringing animal whom he loved dearly, as he did all animals.

"Sorry Rover!" he murmurs, but loud enough for us all to hear; my mother, and we two girls who are clinging, horror stricken to her skirts.

My whole being cries out, with bitter outrage: *What good is sorry?*

Yet, in retrospect, that gruff apology, which was as near as no matter to a sob, seems to me to carry great significance.

4

"YOU HAVE A STAMMER, haven't you?" I shrank from what seemed to me like an accusation. It came from the pursed lips of the teacher in charge of the infant class-room of the village school. My shrinking did not go unnoticed, for she continued in gentler tones: "Like our new King, George V." And she smiled benignly on me. Caught between the shame of having a stammer, and the high honor of being compared with the reigning monarch, I shrank even further from her searching gaze, and from the curious eyes of the other infants in the room.

"Eileen is such a shy little thing, Emmie," she told my mother one day outside the village shop. She called my mother by her Christian name because she had taught her in school too; and I was baffled by the contrast between the joking, genial woman who ruffled my hair while she winked at my mother, and the stern, impatient teacher who could make the whole of the infant class quail under her fury, and who had once smacked me for dropping a stitch of my knitting.

I remember sitting with the hateful green knitting hopelessly entangled on the thick, bone needles, willing

31

the hands of the yellow-faced, roman-figured clock on the wall to pass the half past three mark. Teacher had said that if I made one more mistake with the knitting, she would smack me. Paralyzed with fear and misery, I sat and awaited my doom. Teacher's eyes roamed toward the clock. She began to put her things away in her desk. She found, among her things a square of milk chocolate in purple paper, and, picking it up between her chalky finger and thumb, she popped it furtively into her mouth. Her cheek bulged, her eyes registered the soothing pleasure of the smooth sweetness. Then she saw me. Two red spots appeared in her cheeks, she chewed the chocolate, and with an impatient sigh, darted toward me and grabbed the tangled knitting. Then she took my trembling hand in hers and smacked it sharply several times. The smell of the chocolate on her breath somehow sharpened my anguish.

Perhaps I remember this incident more clearly than many others from my infant days, because Teacher (as we always called her in school) was usually kind to me. Being the type of child who did fairly well at lessons, and who was too shy to make my presence felt more than necessary, I did not often incur the displeasure of my teachers. And even at the tender age of six or seven, I remember being aware while she smacked me for the muddled knitting, that Teacher regretted having made the threat in the first place. But having made it, she had to carry it out.

I remember that she often gave us compositions to write, or drawings to do, centered round a mythical character called Bill. She would give us a sentence, like, "Picking up the ladder, Bill set off up the street, looking from left to right to make sure no one was coming." This, she would say, was to be the first sentence of a story.

Now, get busy and make up the rest. I enjoyed doing this, and never minded whether it was to be a story or a drawing, because I was reasonably good at both. I can still recall the fascination that the tins of colored chalks had for me, with their soft colors and peculiar powdery smell. Our finished efforts, if they were good enough, would be pinned up on the wall for all to see. Once when writing a story about the notorious Bill, I caused him to say: "I've fell down!"

"Now, Eileen," said Teacher, "is this a mistake in *your* grammar, or did you mean Bill, being an ignorant village lad, to talk like that?"

I was confused. I knew I had made the mistake, but what was this about Bill being an "ignorant village lad"? Wasn't I, after all, only a "village girl"?

"I meant him to talk like that," I said, feeling that Teacher had put a subtle temptation in my way. But I felt guilty about that lie for weeks afterwards.

My sister, though just a year older than me, was somewhat slower at her lessons. One day, while reading to Teacher from an infant reader, she stuck on a word.

"Come on, come on! What is it child, what is it?"

Teacher's impatient finger stabbed the offending word.

"Party," blurted out Sylvia in despair.

Teacher sighed ominously, then turned toward where I sat and crooked her chalky finger in a beckoning gesture. Cautiously I approached.

"Tell your sister what this word is."

I looked, and knew at once what it was.

"Pretty," I said reluctantly.

"You see!" gloated Teacher triumphantly, glowering down at my unfortunate sister. "Your little sister can do better than you can!"

What did I feel? Pleasure at her praise, or pity for my sister's humiliation? Perhaps a little of each, though I would like to be able to report that it was all of the latter. At any rate, my fear of and hostility toward Teacher was akin to what I felt for my father. In both cases, though their anger was rarely directed at me but to those around me, yet I reacted emotionally as though I alone were the victim of their violence. The fact that it was not I, personally, who incurred their rage did not alter the degree of my inward terror of them.

The fact that I grew up with a hatred of all violence, so that I cannot to this day watch it even on a television screen without reacting with an actual physical twitch, and that I retained a strong aversion to knitting until I was well into my twenties; and that I have never been able to wear green, or to look with any favor upon it as a furnishing color, may all have some bearing upon those infant days, who can tell!

Mercifully for me, one graduated from the "Little Room" which housed the infants, to the "Big Room" which was for the seniors, when one reached the exalted age of seven. Sylvia, who had already spent a year in the Big Room by virtue of her age, proudly introduced her little sister to the new teacher there.

Miss Beaumont was not of village origin, and we could only assume that she came from the only other place which existed to our childish minds apart from the village—London—that magic place, that other world inhabited by strange creatures who had somehow managed not to be born in one of the fifty or sixty cottages which straggled around our village green. (The village did, in fact, have two greens—Upper Green and Lower Green. The two were divided by a long, narrowly sloping road called Bull Lane. The Lower Greeners were

almost foreigners to us Upper Greeners. They had their
own chapel, and their own village pump. And, of
course, their own pub. But the children of Lower Green
had to climb the long hill to come to school each day, and
this gave us the edge on them. The parish church was
almost halfway in between, but even this was nearer to
"us" than "them"!)

When I hear people say that their attitude toward
poetry and literature—especially the works of Shakespeare—was warped by having to "do" them at school,
and that it would be much better if we could all discover
these treasures for ourselves, I want to cry out in protest.
My own love and appreciation for all that is good in our
heritage of literature came to me, I am sure, as a direct
result of teachers who themselves had a deep love for the
English language. These women stand out for me in my
memory as major influences on my mind, and I shall
always be grateful to them.

Miss Beaumont was an individualist. I knew that as
soon as I set eyes on her, though obviously, at the age of
seven I would not have expressed it in those words, or in
any words at all. I simply knew when I entered that Big
Room for the first time, and saw Miss Beaumont warm-
ing her tweed clad bottom by the tall guard which surrounded the open fireplace by the teacher's desk that
here was someone in whose care I would be "safe"; that
here was space to breathe, to be myself without having to
be constantly looking over my shoulder for the enemy.

Often our English lessons would consist entirely of
Miss Beaumont reading to us aloud. Sometimes it was
from Rudyard Kipling's *Just So Stories*, sometimes from
Alice in Wonderland, or Kenneth Graham's *Wind in the
Willows*. When Miss Beaumont was reading, she forgot
us altogether. She would walk up and down by her desk,

gesticulating with her hands and arms, chuckling to
herself as she became first the magnificent Toad of
Toadhall, then the deliciously lazy, comfort-loving Mole,
or sensible, man-of-the-world Ratty. Her eyes would
sparkle with delight as she declaimed the joys of "mess-
ing about on the river," or of roaring through the country
lanes in Toad's wickedly high-powered car.

She encouraged us to read for ourselves, made sure
that the bookshelf was equipped with attractive, read-
able books, and set aside at least one period each week
for "silent reading." She saw each child as an individual,
and was quick to spot the essential character and poten-
tial of the seemingly difficult ones. I well remember the
infinite pains she took with one boy whom everyone else
had given up as a hopeless case. She really loved that
boy, and somehow her attitude toward him transformed
him in our eyes from an irritating, mischief-making adolescent into someone popular and lovable. I cannot re
member exactly how she went about encouraging me,
too, drawing me out, building up my confidence in my
own ability, but I only know that she did it. She was
patient, she was understanding, she was warmly ap-
proachable. But at the same time she could be strict and
uncompromising in the standards of behavior she set for
the class.

A single incident, the only occasion when I remember
incurring her displeasure stands out in my mind. I was
getting ready to go home in the girl's cloakroom which
adjoined the Big Room, and as I was with two or three
other girls, and we were all in a giggly mood, I felt the
sudden urge to do something daringly outrageous—an
urge with which I was not really very familiar! On the
other side of the classroom door, we could hear Miss
Beaumont coaching one of the boys for his scholarship

exam, for which he was due to sit shortly. Creeping up to the door, and no doubt wishing to impress the other girls, I put my mouth to the keyhole of the door and made a very rude noise. Then immediately full of horror at what I had done, I scampered with the others out of the cloakroom and into the playground running for home. I remember thinking, hopefully: "Even if she runs out to see who did it, she'll never guess it was me, because it just isn't the kind of thing I would *ever* do!"

But Miss Beaumont, justly irritated by the rude, mindless intrusion on her private coaching lesson, did run out. And what is more, she immediately called out in an unusually shrill voice:

"Eileen Funston—see me in the morning!"

At once I was consumed by guilt, remorse and fear. How had my beloved teacher known it was me? Why not one of the other girls, whom, she must have known, were far more capable of the foul deed than I was. And what would happen to me in the morning? Would she smack me, as she had been known to do to other girls who exasperated her (unruly boys she caned). Would she denounce me verbally, maybe even publicly.... I couldn't bear the thought of any of this.

When I arrived home, I was already sick with misery and dread. I roamed alone in the kitchen garden, head bent, hands in pockets, trying to think of a way of escape from the impending doom. I knew I was a coward, and I despised myself for it. Could I make myself ill so that I wouldn't have to go to school at all next day? Or so that Miss Beaumont would take pity on me and let me off?

After a sleepless night, tomorrow came at last, and I dragged my reluctant legs over the meadows and across the green to school. Olive, my closest friend advised:

"Don't go in school yet. Stay out here and skip with us.

She'll come out and fetch you if she wants you. But more than likely she's forgotten all about it already—you see!"

Olive was right. After a bit Miss Beaumont did come out into the playground, as she usually did about five minutes before nine o'clock. She stood there for awhile and watched us girls skipping, and she was close enough to see clearly that I was amongst the skippers. Then she raised her whistle to her lips and blew a long blast. Next minute the whole playground full of children dropped their balls and ropes and surged into school. Miss Beaumont said the prayers for the day, then proceeded with the lessons. Not a word did she say about the previous afternoon's events. Nor did she give any sign to me, then or later, that she remembered anything about it. If possible, I loved her even more dearly after that.

She knows I didn't mean it! She knows it wasn't the real me that did it. I shall never forget it . . .

And I never have. The knowledge of that teacher's sensitive comprehension of me as a whole person did more for me than any reprimand or punishment could ever have done.

5

SYLVIA AND I were sitting up in the double bed that we shared in the back bedroom, reading. My mother's footsteps clattered up the wooden, carpetless back stairs which led up from the kitchen, and we raised our eyes from our story books to see what see wanted.

Mother stood regarding us for a moment in silence, and then she said:

"There's very bad news. War has just been declared."

Her lips quivered and her eyes were bright with tears as she sat down on the edge of our bed.

Sylvia said: "Will Dad have to go and be a soldier?"

Mother shook her head, and her face returned to normal.

"No, farmers don't have to go. They're needed to go on producing food for the country."

"That's all right, then, isn't it?" And we returned to our story books.

The war was to drastically change our quiet village life. Before long a colony of army huts appeared in the meadow beyond the stackyard, and among the haystacks a cement platform was built to support the

generator which was to activate the giant search-lights
later to be stationed at the back of the camp. Army lorries
trundled through the quiet lanes, and khaki-clad soldiers were everywhere. My sister and I were excited. All
at once there was the unfamiliar, exhilarating sense of
not knowing what was going to happen next. The un-
easy voices of the grownups rumbled on over our heads.
We neither knew nor cared what it was all about.

Not long afterwards, Mother came to us again with the
same unaccustomed expression of suppressed excitement and apprehension on her face.

"If I tell you a secret, will you promise to keep it?"
We nodded. What now?

"I might—I just *might* be going to have a baby."

"Oh, Mum, when, when? Will it be a boy?"

"How do I know, sillies? And remember, it isn't for
sure yet, so don't go talking about it at school."

Her eyes looked suddenly stern, as if she'd only just
thought of this possibility. I wonder, looking back, why
she told us before she was sure. I can only assume she
couldn't keep the secret to herself! There was nobody
else to tell, unless she walked into the village to tell one of
my aunts.

At school we chanted to our friends: "We've got a
secret, we've got a secret."

"Your Mum's going to have a baby." It was Olive, who
was a bit of a know-all. We stopped in our tracks, horrified. How could she possibly know?

"Don't be daft!" I hissed in a mad attempt to put things
right. After all, I told myself, she *is* wrong: the secret is
that Mum *might*, not *is*.

Mum confirmed the news a little later, but we still
weren't to tell.

"We've got a secret, we've got a secret." we chanted.

"I know, I know," sighed Olive. "Your Mum *might* be going to have a baby." (We must have put her right some time in the intervening period, but I don't remember doing it.)

"That secret was silver—this one is gold!" This was me, holding desperately on to the last vestige of one-upmanship. The gold, I told myself, is *knowing*. *Hoping* was only silver. But both, of course, were precious in their own way.

Mother thought it was a good chance to take a deep breath and introduce us to the facts of life. Or did we ask questions? At any rate, I remember that she calmly got out the Bible one day and began to read us the story of Elizabeth, and how the babe leapt in her womb. We knew the story, of course. No one had ever explained it to us, nor had we found it necessary to ask. We just accepted it, as we did everying else in the Bible. So it was the most natural thing in the world to be told that our new baby brother was leaping inside my mother's womb, too.

But a thought suddenly occurred to Sylvia.

"How did it get there, then?"

Mother got up and put the Bible back on the shelf.

"That," she said, "you will find out later, when you're old enough to understand."

Besides the war and the news of the coming baby, something else happened to us that year. I went up to our young minister after the Thursday night meeting of our Young Sower's League and told him that I wanted to "give my heart to Jesus." The thing that stands out most clearly in my memory about this event is the look of pure joy which transformed his face as I told him. His dark eyes shone, and the very skin of his forehead seemed to glow with light.

On the way home, Sylvia said: "Why didn't you tell me you were going to do that?"

I couldn't really see what it had to do with her.

"Why?"

"Well, I would have done it too, silly."

"But you still can!"

We were approaching the stackyard where a very fierce cockerel would often jump out and run at us as we passed. I was terrified of him. Today, however, I approached his lair with boldness.

"I'm not afraid!" I laughed. "Isn't it marvelous, I'm not afraid!"

Sylvia looked doubtful. "Why aren't you?"

"Because I've got Jesus in my heart! Don't you see. He's with me all the time now, so I needn't be afraid anymore!"

The minister's wife gave me a little gold-covered book by Frances Ridley Havergal, with daily readings in simple prose. It was called "Little Pillows," and I treasured it dearly, keeping it under my pillow and reading it faithfully every night. Sylvia, who had in the meantime told the minister that she, too, wanted to give her heart to Jesus, came home proudly bearing a similar booklet called "Morning Bells," intended, of course, to be read at the opposite end of the day from my "Little Pillows."

I hesitate to say any more at all about this, because although the little books bore the inscription: "Presented to (in my case) Eileen Funston, on the day she gave her heart to the Lord Jesus," subsequent years were to show that I may not have fully understood, at nine years of age, what the giving of the "heart," a term so familiar to Christians, really meant. I did not really know about self-love, about sin, about the secret inroads of self-will and self-deception to which we are all increasingly sub-

ject, until the innocence of childhood gave way to the
awakening voices of adolescence. My heart, it seems to
me, was not yet mine to give. Or maybe I am wrong.
Who am I to say that the nine-year-old girl who defied
the angry cockerel in Jesus' name had not that very day
taken the first step along the road to the heavenly city,
where shone the beckoning spring of life. God alone
knows the precise moment at which the rebel self, which
is really the heart of man, truly surrenders to the unseen
magnetism of divine love.

It was not long after this that Miss Beaumont said, one
afternoon, that she was going up to the parish church
immediately after school, and anyone who wished to go
with her might do so. Needless to say, I was among the
small group of girls who went. I can't remember what
was the purpose of the visit. Perhaps there wasn't one.
Miss Beaumont was given to doing unpredictable and
seemingly motiveless things. It was one of the reasons
why I loved her.

I remember the moment when we entered the doorway of the beautiful fifteenth century building and stood
looking toward the altar at the far end. The chapel, with
its plain windows, yellow varnished pews and tortoise
stone, seemed very far away. I looked down at the ancient stone beneath my feet, at the lovely colors of the
stained glass windows and the gleaming brass of the
lectern, and I was in a foreign land. Even the smell was
different. A foreign land, yet I did not feel like a
foreigner. At my elbow, Miss Beaumont said: "Would
you like to go into the children's corner and pray?"

I nodded. Where were the others who had come?
Nearby, I suppose. But I was alone in the sweet-smelling
silence, and time stood still. There was a little prayer
desk, with a blue embroidered hassock to kneel on and

an open, illustrated Bible on the top. Without a moment's hesitation, I knelt down. In chapel we never knelt to pray, but sat hunched on the pew with our heads bent. In chapel there were no crosses to be seen, no choir stalls, no altar. By implication we were taught that chapel was right, church slightly off-center, and therefore to be politely avoided. Chapel people believed that there were some things about church that were just plain wrong— like having crosses, which left you in danger of breaking the second commandment, and bowing down to a graven image; and like the altar, with its suggestion of the need for a sacrifice—which, of course, had been done away with by Christ's once-and-for-all sacrifice for sin upon the cross. There were other things which we children *gathered* were wrong just because the church had always done them and the chapel never had. Into this category came the singing of psalms and kneeling for prayer.

But I knelt in the children's corner, and I looked at the golden cross embroidered on the little altar cloth without a twinge of guilt. And to my surprise, the Jesus I loved was there, filling my heart with quiet joy.

Miss Beaumont said gently, "We'd better go." And I tore myself away from the lovely presence and went out through the ancient fourteenth century doorway into the sunlit churchyard beyond.

6

WE ARRIVED HOME from school one dinner time to find our father cutting slices of meat off a cold joint. A loaf of bread was on the table and some butter. My mother was nowhere to be seen. Dad mumbled something about Mum not feeling very well, and we were to eat our dinners as quickly as possible and get back to school. Why wasn't Mum well, we pursued? He finally admitted that the baby looked like it was on the way, and that we were to be good girls and get back to school as quick as possible. We gobbled our dinner and escaped willingly.

Afternoon school dragged, and Sylvia was impatient to get home and see our new brother. It never occurred to us that it might be a sister instead of a brother, and Sylvia at this time was bursting with excitement. She loved babies, and had always longed for one "of our own." I was not so sure. I ran home with her that afternoon with a show of eagerness, but an unnamed dread made my legs seem heavy. What was happening to my mother? How could the "leaping" baby suddenly leap right out and be in our house when we got there?

In my memory, it seems as if the smell of Dettol greeted us while we were still crossing the meadow. When we crept in the back door, the house was quiet, and my mother lay in the "middle" downstairs room. With beating hearts we tip-toed in. There lay our mother, pale upon the pillow, and there in the cradle by the bed lay our little brother. My sister rushed to look at him, but I hung back. There was something about the room—the smell of it, the feel of it, that seemed to repel me. There was something essentially physical about everything around me, and it made me want to close up my senses as a flower closes its petals. And yet there was another element, too—an element that was both earthy and unearthy at the same time, a kind of calm after the storm. It made my mother seem very far away like a half-drowned stranger washed up on a distant beach. I took a quick look at the red, furry head in the cradle, and slipped out of the room, out of the house into the familiar freshness of the September afternoon.

About this time, government officials began to appear in the village knocking on doors. They knocked on our door and started asking questions about the number of rooms in our house. They left with a warning that parts of London were being evacuated, and that we would have to take some people in. It must have been a tremendous upheaval for my mother, turning the upstairs rooms into living quarters for another family, deciding what to leave up there, what to bring down. Our lovely peaceful home was changed overnight into a noisy boarding house. None of the families stayed long, because most of them could not bear the quietness of village life.

"How can you stand it?" the women asked my mother. "How can you stay here, buried alive, for years on end? We'd go crazy if we had to stay here much longer! We'd rather have the bombs!"

We had sympathized with the poor things when we had thought of them living in London, with bombs falling around them, and houses burning, and people they knew being killed everyday, but we were relieved when our home was finally our own again, and the evacuees were all gone.

One Wednesday afternoon, Miss Beaumont said that instead of our usual English lesson, she was going to give us each an exercise book, and that we were to begin to write a story. We were to write for the whole of the English lesson, but were to remember that we were only writing the beginning of the story, because the story, when finished would fill the whole book. We would go on writing it every week until it was finished and the book was full. I still remember the pang of pleasure I felt as I reached out my hand eagerly for the new, ruled exercise book.

It was the first time I had consciously thought of becoming a writer. I had always loved writing "compositions" as we called them, and story making came easily to me from infancy. I loved the sound of words, and the sight of them on the printed page. To be asked to take a whole glorious pile of them and to sort them out like pieces of a jig-saw puzzle and build them into a story, a story long enough to fill a whole book, was heady stuff. I couldn't begin fast enough.

Around me, the other children chewed their pens and sighed, scratched a few lines, and sighed again. But I was up, up and away. My story was about a horse, a much-loved horse, whose owner had fallen into debt and was forced to sell him. On the day that he was due to be taken to market, the horse, nuzzling sadly in his stable, touched the secret spring of an old wood panel in the wall. The panel slid back to reveal a bag of gold. With the bag between his teeth, our hero burst open the stable door and galloped off to find his master. The bag of gold, of course, contained more than enough to save the situation, and horse and owner lived happily ever after. Looking back, I think I recognize shades of *Black Beauty*, with a few handfuls of *School Girl Annual* thrown in for good measure. But it was my very own creation, all the same, and I wrote my name on the cover of the exercise book with "age nine years." The book was freely illustrated by the author with pencil drawings throughout. Miss Beaumont read it with obvious pleasure, wrote "I like this story very much" on the last page in red pencil, and handed it back to me with a warm smile.

"Time we started preparing you for the scholarship," she said.

"But my parents aren't sure if they want me to, Miss."

"Nonsense. Of course you must. Ridiculous."

My parents had several reasons for their reluctance to let me try for a scholarship, though it was the only way you would get a high school education in those days, unless your parents were rich enough to pay fees. Herts and Essex High School for Girls was eleven miles away at Bishops Stortford. We were in the second year of the war, and although few bombs had fallen near us, the thought of sending me to school in a *town* filled them with fear. After all, all sorts of terrible things happened in towns. Also, even if I passed, there would be a lot of incidental expenses—uniform, sports equipment and so on. The war was only just beginning to bring the financial boom to farming that was to arrive later, bringing with it comforts and luxuries unheard of in our home before. But Miss Beaumont won the day.

On the day of the exam, my mother dressed me in a mustard yellow jumper and a brown skirt with straps that crossed over at the back. She had made them both herself, and the knowledge that I looked "right" in them—my first conscious recognition of this feminine need!—helped me to face the eight mile car ride into Saffron Walden. I always felt sick in cars, and this time was no exception. I staggered into the examination room feeling white and shaky. But the nausea passed, and I was soon working away at an English paper.

After thirty-five years, I can still remember one question which filled me with suspicion. We were asked to fill in the missing letter in an acrostic. Sideways it read: RI...ER, downwards it was simply E...E. My immediate instinct was to fill a V into the space, making it River and Eve. But this seemed too easy. Then I remembered. Examiners sometimes put in trick questions to see how quick you were. If I put a V, they would think I didn't know that Eve was not an ordinary noun, but only stood for a girl's name, or an abbreviation for "evening." Yet if I put a Y, making it read EYE downwards, it would then read RIYER crossways. I had never heard of such a word, but that didn't mean to say no such word existed. Better to risk this than the shame of falling for a catch question. So I put a Y.

My mother had advised me to use as many long words as I could when I wrote my essay.

"Words like 'majority' or 'minority,' or . . ." she couldn't think of any more. For my essay I had to write a letter from a farmer complaining about week-end picnickers who had damaged his property. This was just up my street. My father often went out to yell at timid townsfolk who had dared to set foot on his land in search of a quiet resting spot! And here was my chance to use one of my mother's long words!

"The majority of my fences have been broken down," I wrote grandly, "to say nothing of the damage done to my haystacks and my growing corn...."

Anyway, I passed. And the summer was spent in a state of feverish excitement as I prepared to enter the magic world of School Girls' Annual and Angela Brazil. Or so I thought.

Miss Beaumont left the village school at about this time, and I was sad to see her go, but as I was due to leave myself at the end of term, I was not too troubled. Her place was taken by a stern Anglican lady lay-reader, who most of the time dressed in a dark habit. She was helped by a lady companion, a mousy, gray-clad figure, who assisted on the practical side, helping us girls with our sewing and weaving. I was shaken out of my cocoon of complacency, my cozy sense of being approved, even loved, by Miss Beaumont, when I realized that these two stern ladies saw in me nothing but a bothersome girl who didn't know how to knit ribbing without making a mistake, and whose sewing was pitiful.

"You are the worst seamstress in the school!" snapped one of them on the day I made an especially poor attempt at stitching up a green and yellow pinafore. I was stunned. No teacher had spoken to me like that for years. Inwardly, humiliated, I nevertheless tossed my head, figuratively, if not actually. What did I care? I was going to a school where I could *choose* between needlework and art, so there! No doubt the new teacher's lack of approval was good for me, but that term dragged its feet rather, and I left without the slightest twinge of regret, in spite of the happy years spent in the Big Room with my beloved Miss Beaumont.

I recently read of a Yorkshire headmaster who used to

say he divided the young into thought-makers and thing-makers. Quite rightly, he never made any distinction of superiority or inferiority between the two types, but felt it was helpful to remember that most children did fall roughly into the two categories. Perhaps other teachers would do well to take this into account. The Marthas and the Marys, and the Peters and the Johns, have always been with us, and always will.

As my infant teacher gave me a long-term hatred of knitting, so this new senior teacher killed any taste I had for sewing. Not until I was able to approach dressmaking in an entirely new way, that is to say as a creative art rather than as a technical skill, did I ever pick up a needle again. Then it was as a young married woman, when, having once tasted the joys of designing my own clothes, choosing my own styles, colors and materials, I went on to make practically everything I wore, and did the same for my children. But at school I decided that sewing was not for me. Unconsciously I dubbed myself a "thought-maker" and stuck to it. And basically, I suppose that is what I am.

Three clearly etched pictures stand out in my mind, and two of them must have taken place during those pre-high school days. The first one shows me sitting up in bed reading the story of Solomon. I am fascinated by the fact that Solomon, given the choice of anything in the world, chose simply the gift of wisdom. I sit for a while, lost in thought. Then, kneeling up on my pillow I grasp the brass bedhead in my two hands. Resting my head on my clasped hands, I pray fervently for the gift of wisdom. Childish presumption? I don't know. But kneeling there I feel a simple assurance that God has heard me.

In the second picture I am walking with a school friend over the green toward the school. We are approaching the cricket pitch, when suddenly I turn to the friend and ask:

"Do you ever stop and ask yourself if you are perfectly happy—blissfully and completely happy without a shadow to spoil it anywhere?"

I see her jaw drop, her eyes look scared.

I say, "Because I do, often!"

She murmurs an excuse, and then turns and runs across the cricket pitch as though I have just announced that I have the plague. And in retrospect, I can't say I blame her!

The third incident must have taken place later, in my early teens. I am cycling to our grocer, three miles away in the next village. As I freewheel down a hill, a sense of unaccountable exhilaration which has nothing to do with the bicycle, or the feeling of the wind on my face, wells up in me. I shut my eyes and throw back my head so that my hair streams behind me; and I pray aloud that God will never take away from me my sense of sin.

By the time I left for high school, Sylvia was totally absorbed in my baby brother. No one had ever suggested that she should sit for a scholarship, and she never wanted to anyway. When, four years after the birth of Anthony John, a second little brother was born, my sister was delighted. She left school around this time, and for several years stayed at home to help my mother with the two little boys. It was not until she was eighteen that she ventured outside the village, and then it was to look after someone else's little boys in a London suburb.

7

I NOW EMBARKED on what was probably the most formative period of my life, my high school days. As soon as I entered the vast, light, elegantly designed buildings, I felt that I was breathing a different air. The long polished corridors gleamed ahead of me like roads to the promised land. The huge square hall in which four hundred girls assembled every morning for prayers, was hung all round with wooden panels on which were engraved the names of previous scholars who had gone on to graduate at one of the universities then open to women. The details of their degrees were written large for all to see. An incentive to spur us on to similar heights, no doubt.

The hall, which was surrounded by long windows on three sides, had a wide stage on the third, above which ran a gallery. The upper wall of the gallery was decorated with white stone grecian frescoes, and a door led out of the gallery at either end to the rest of the upper story. At first I felt that I would never find my way around the maze of classrooms and corridors. Even Angela Brazil's fascinating Boarding Schools paled into insignificance beside this!

Everywhere I looked there were girls in uniforms, which were basically beige and sky blue, and there was not, of course, a boy in sight! When later I visited the boys' grammar school a few miles away, I realized that it was the all-female population of our school which accounted for its well-kept appearance. In the boys' school I found the same inkstained desks, grubby walls and dingy paintwork with which I had grown familiar in the village school. At the girls' school I felt a sense of belonging. No more rough, jostling, shouting boys with their dirty talk and bullying ways! It seemed too good to be true!

I had to travel by bus to and from school each day, and as the journey took an hour this meant leaving home soon after half past seven each morning and arriving home well after five. For the first few weeks I was sick every morning. But the bus driver soon became a friend of mine, and kept me in the front seat near the door so that I could hang out in moments of dire necessity. I tried everything—eating no breakfast, eating on the bus, eating as soon as I arrived at school, but no system really worked. To this day the taste of tomato sandwiches reminds me of those early high school days and those miserable bus rides through the winding country lanes in the semi-darkness of a winter's morning.

My love of English and my urge to express myself by the written word soon blossomed and developed under the guiding hand of Miss Pearse, the headmistress, and an English teacher called Mrs. Appleby. Mrs. Appleby was as different as she could be from Miss Beaumont; she was fair, gentle and dreamy, while Miss Beaumont had been stout, tweedy and outspoken. Miss Beaumont had romped her way through English lessons with an enthusiasm almost bordering on greed, and she swept along with her anyone who happened to get caught up in the spell. Mrs. Appleby led us gently down the paths of aesthetic appreciation, opening up to us with her delicate touch, the gateways to wider literary delights. Keats, Shelley and the war poets; Shakespeare, Robert Louis Stevenson and Dickens, the Bronte sisters and Jane Austen. I entered a world which took my breath away at almost every turn.

Not that I enjoyed everything we read. Jane Austen seemed to me inexpressibly dry and dull. Dickens, at times, I found tedious. But when Mrs. Appleby read Shelley's "Ode to the West Wind," I thrilled to the delicious anguish of the poet's cry:

> 'O, lift me as a wave, a leaf, a cloud!
> I fall upon the thorns of life! I bleed!
> A heavy weight of hours has chained and bowed
> One too like thee—tameless, and swift and proud!

What did I know at twelve or thirteen, of this kind of despair? Yet from somewhere deep within there came the echo, or the forboding, or simply the instinctive knowledge of the essential aloneness of the human spirit. And in a timeless moment, the forerunner, maybe, of a good many more such moments, I simultaneously embraced and shrank from that knowledge.

When Mrs. Appleby introduced us to Francis Thompson's "Hound of Heaven," I understood for the first time the meaning of man's true plight, as I witnessed the soul's flight from a pursuing God, the relentless lover. I recognized here the mystery of divine love, and the ageless conflict at the heart of everyman as he both yearns for and flees from the very giver of life himself. The poetry tore me apart with delight. I was ravished, enchanted by the unbearable beauty of it:

> *But if one little casement parted wide*
> *The gust of His approach would clash it to.*
> *Fear wist not to evade, as Love wist to pursue.*
> *Across the margent of the world I fled,*
> *And troubled the gold gateway of the stars,*
> *Smiting for shelter on their clanged bars....*

Yet alongside these poetic fancies went some very human fancies too. My thoughts were beginning to turn to another kind of love. It pleased me to think that the gentle, dreamy-eyed Mrs. Appleby had a husband waiting to take her in his arms when she arrived home after a grueling day spent trying to instill a little culture into us raw schoolgirls. I wondered what he looked like. Was he as handsome as she was lovely? I never saw him, so I never knew. But the thought of their life together fed my adolescent imagination pleasurably.

One or two girls in my class had boyfriends already, to my secret envy. Meantime, I had to make the most of what little masculine admiration came my way from the soldiers in the camp at the back of the farm. Girls who talked to soldiers, especially young girls, always caused a great deal of gossip in the village, so one had to be careful. But one could enjoy unashamedly the pleasure of waving from the back of the school bus to the cheering soldiers who hung out of the back of passing army lorries. Sometimes one of us would cry: "A convoy!" And up we would all kneel along the back seat, where we usually sat, and start waving to the soldiers as the lorries zoomed past. If one lorry got stuck behind us, we would amuse ourselves by picking out the young, good-looking ones.

"Mine's the tall fair one second from the left!"

"No, he's mine! I saw him first! You can have the little ginger one with the cheeky blue eyes!"

The soldiers would be up to the same kind of lark. They would pick their girl out and point to her, without any regard for the feelings of the rest of us. Being a blue-eyed blonde, I was sometimes the target of the pointing finger, but more often than not it would be my dark-haired cousin's turned up nose and twinkling brown eyes they went for. In those days I was very overweight, having suddenly started to expand at about the age of ten, and I was convinced that had the soldiers been able to see the whole of me, instead of just my head and shoulders, I wouldn't have stood a chance!

American airmen came to man the airfield which had been built a couple of miles outside our village, and to us girls they seemed like gods from Olympus. Tall, blonde, good-looking (they couldn't *all* have been, but for some reason that's the way I remember them!) and outrageously flirtatious, they became the chief topic of our conversation for a while. With their easy good manners and charm, they seemed to embody all our ideas of romance, and when one of them began to lay in wait for me on my way to and from the Girl Guide Hut, I didn't know whether to be pleased or scared. One day he insisted on giving me a ride on his cross-bar. Too scared to refuse, I submitted to riding through the village perched precariously on the cross-bar in my Girl Guide uniform. But an aunt of mine made it clear to me next day that she had seen me, and after that I doggedly avoided him.

One day when I was driving my father's tractor in a cornfield, I saw an American soldier with his landgirl fiancée standing together at the edge of the field watching the progress of the reaping. The soldier was smoking a pipe, and as he turned to look across the field, he inadvertently touched the cheek of the girl with the hot bowl of his pipe. She winced and put her hand up to her face, and he immediately took the pipe from his mouth and bent to kiss the sore spot on her cheek. It was all over in a moment, but it left a lasting impression on my young mind. I had never seen a man showing that kind of tenderness to a woman before, and I said to myself, *That's the kind of man I'm going to marry.* And so I did.

Some Italian prisoners were housed in a cottage just outside the village, and they were allowed to cycle freely to and from the farms where they worked. One of these prisoners used to stop and chat with me if he met me along the village road, and I took pity on him. Exiled from his home, I felt sure that he must long for human companionship. I talked to him about his family, his country, his life way back in pre-war Italy, and after one or two such chats he, too, began to "lie in wait" for me.

I knew my parents wouldn't approve of such goings on, though I was innocent enough not to understand why. Apart from the fact that the Italians were our enemies, compatriots of the hated Mussolini, any contact with older men was naturally suspect. I began to meet my Italian friend in quiet spots in the country lanes, making sure no one was looking on. But I told my school friend about it, and she, being far more sophisticated than I, encouraged me to think of the whole thing as a romantic adventure. She thought of various ways to deceive my parents, and before long what had begun innocently enough became a hole-in-the-corner affair which filled me with feelings of guilt. I knew my parents would be furious if they found out, so without actually telling them any lies, I hid my movements from them with subtle deceits.

Eventually, my mother did find out—in a village the size of ours it was, of course, inevitable—and a terrible storm ensued. I begged her not to tell my father, and until I drew from her some kind of promise that she would not, felt close enough to real terror to contemplate running away from home.

Later, Sylvia told me how my mother had quizzed her about the affair, asking her if I had ever been into the cottage where the men lived, *or anything like that.* I was horrified that an innocent friendship had been so besmirched—although later, of course, I was able to deeply sympathize with my mother's anguish. But my guilt was increased unbearably, and I wrote to my mother a letter in which I tried desperately to put things right. I pushed the letter into her hand before I left for school one day, and that night as she thanked me for it, she burst into tears. No more was said, and my father never knew about any of it.

Meantime, my school work was suffering, and the emotional preoccupations of my mind were crippling my progress badly. Instead of being at the top of my class, as I had been in the early days at high school, I slid down to below the halfway line. My headmistress sent for me and tried to find out the reason for it all. Was there trouble at home? Had I got something on my mind? She was so disappointed in me; she had thought me to be university material—and now look at what had happened to me! I looked and was deeply ashamed. The gentle, but stern voice of Miss Pearse went like an arrow to my heart.

I knew I had come to a crossroads.

8

A TRAVELING EVANGELIST came to the village one day and asked my father if he could put his tent and caravan in one of our meadows. The news soon spread among the children in the village that there were going to be special meetings with singing and stories, in the big tent in the meadow every evening. Sylvia and I went along and sat with the other teenagers on the back bench. We sat there with the grass growing around our feet, while the evangelist's wife played a little portable harmonium, and the evangelist himself played a concertina. Many of the choruses we sang were well-known to most of us already, because we sang them in Sunday school, and at the Young Sower's meetings on Thursday nights.

> There's a way back to God
> From the dark paths of sin
> There's a door that is open
> And you may go in
> At Calvary's cross is where you begin
> When you come as a sinner to Jesus!

One night when the evangelist was speaking, I felt something inside me open up—not eagerly, as when I had "given my heart" to Jesus at the age of nine, but painfully. I was alarmed by the thought that the "paths of sin" were dark in spite of the fact that they didn't seem dark while you were on them. When I had sneaked out for my secret meetings with the Italian prisoner, I hadn't really stopped to think of the wrongness of what I was doing. Although the actual meetings with the man were, from my point of view, entirely devoid of any sexual connotation, there was more to them than a simple, compassionate desire to give him a little comfort and companionship. I had come to see the whole thing in a romantic light, and egged on by my unscrupulous school friend, began to enjoy the clandestine nature of the affair. Deceiving my mother became all part of the game, and the "path" on which I trod looked, not dark, but lit with the allure of adventure.

Looking back on it, I was appalled by the suffering I had caused my mother, and by the thought that I, whom everyone seemed to regard as above "That kind of thing," should be capable of such behavior. I thought of other traits in my character which I would not want (for example) Mrs. Appleby to know about. The way I quarrelled with my sister and spoke sharp, hurtful words to her sometimes; my lack of consideration for my mother in her over-worked, over-burdened life; my secret hostility toward my father, in spite of his obvious affection for me. I saw a dark side to my nature which had never looked dark to me before. And what frightened me was the knowledge that I had no control over it; that it could even make itself look "light" to me so that I would not recognize it for what it was.

But here was the evangelist telling me that the heart of man is like that. That he is born with the germ of sin already in him, and that he walks in darkness because of it. I already knew that Jesus had come into the world to save mankind from this condition; that his death upon the cross was to atone for my sins, but this knowledge had not, until that moment in the tent, reached the heart of me.

"Now," explained the evangelist, "if you will tell Jesus that you know yourself to be a sinner, and really mean it, he will come right into your life and take control. Not only does the blood of Jesus cleanse us from all sin, but through him we can have the victory over sin from the day that he makes us his own."

I didn't stop to argue that I was "his own" already. The words of the evangelist struck like an arrow to the very point of my need. As the painful "opening up" process took place, so the Spirit to God himself came pouring in and I was "born again" to newness of life. I had taken that little tin jugful of self-love, as Sylvia and I did when we fetched water from the pump, and poured it out in blind faith into the bottomless well of God's love. And now the spring of joy, the life-giving water of salvation, was released in me for all eternity.

I ran home across the meadow, feeling as though my heart would burst. All the beauty I loved so much—the burnished gold, upturned faces of the buttercups, the sound of the grasshopper in the sweet-smelling grass at my feet, the blue haze on the distant woodland, the blue bowl of the summer sky above me—all these, the works of his hand, raised their voices in a paean of praise to their creator and mine. Life itself opened up before me in pristine beauty. It was a new beginning.

In his book *The Pursuit of God*, Tozer has expressed so well what happens to us when God invades our lives with his love:

"Being made in his image, we have within us the

capacity to know him. In our sins we lack only the power. The moment the Spirit has quickened us to life in regeneration, our whole being senses its kinship to God and leaps up in joyous recognition. That is the heavenly birth without which we cannot see the Kingdom of God. It is, however, not an end but as inception, for now begins the glorious pursuit, the heart's happy exploration of the infinite riches of the Godhead...."

I had just won a Bible from Young Sower's League for some marathon Bible knowledge test that I had taken. On the flyleaf I now wrote a text which was to take me through the next two years of high school, back to my position near the top of my class, and through many another victory outside the academic field:

I can do all things through Christ which strengtheneth me.

It seemed to me that my father changed from that time on, though maybe the change was primarily in me. He became more mellow, humbler, gentler toward his family and to those outside. I would talk fairly freely with him about the Bible, which he loved and revered, and about the truths which formed the religious background to all our lives. As the years went by, my hostility evaporated along with my fear of him. Yet, if I am to be honest, I must record that something remained, like a deep scar, on the back of my mind. It seems that the first seven years of our lives are so deeply impressionable, that however much we may strive to reverse the effects of the emotional experiences of those years, we can never really do so. It is the wounds received during those early years that take the longest to heal.

I passed the general schools certificate, gaining a high enough standard in my seven subjects to exempt me from sitting my matriculation exam. This meant that I could, if I wished, apply for entry to a university, though I would need, of course, to do a further two years' study in the sixth forms first.

But did I want to go to a university? My parents said it was up to me. I was torn between the pursuit of knowledge and my hunger for "real life." I had loved my school days, but the lure of the world outside, with all that it promised—a quality which I loosely labelled "experience"—was stronger. Two more years at school, followed by several years at a university, did not, at that time, seem to be a very inviting prospect. In vain my headmistress tried to persuade me, telling me what a waste it was not to take my English studies further.

"At least stay on in the sixth form," she begged. "In my experience girls always say later that the two years spent in the sixth forms taught them more than the other five years put together." What did I want to do anyway, she wanted to know.

I said I wanted to write.

"Well then..." she spread out her pale hands in exasperation. "What better preparation for that than a university course in English?"

I did not say so, but I remember feeling that the best preparation would be a course in *living*.

Sometimes now, I regret not having taken Miss Pearse's advice. At other times I wonder. In any case, a life given over to the control of God can surely never, at anytime, call into question the course it took. For he alone knows best what kind of preparation is needed to fit us for the tasks he has for us to do, and what the world calls excellence may not, in fact, be God's excellence at all.

I won the form prize the year I left Herts and Essex

High School for Girls. I asked for a copy of the collected poems of Francis Thompson. Shortly before my six-teenth birthday, I was baptized in the village chapel, and afterwards I wrote a long epic poem, constructed after the style of my beloved *Hound of Heaven*. It was called *Second Daybreak*, and when I gave it to our minister to read, he suggested that I send it up to a religious weekly to see if they would publish it. They did, first writing to ask me for a photo of myself to go with it. The poem filled a whole page of the paper, and was to lead to some interesting developments in my personal life. As poetry it was probably poor stuff, but as the expression of a young girl's heart as she faced the unknown path ahead, it must have had something of value. The last few lines went like this:

> *And as the waters closed above my head*
> *And darkness for a moment veiled my form*
> *I heard the words the great Paul once had said,*
> *"Buried with Him in Baptism." So I rose*
> *And with my Saviour's helping hand I reached*
> *That farther shore, now quite prepared to meet*
> *Fresh trials and temptations. I beseeched*
> *My Lord to make me "more than conqueror."*
> *The great wide road lay open at my feet;*
> *The second great "day" of my life had dawned;*
> *It was the voice of my new self which beat:*
> *"I can do all things through Christ, which*
>   *strengtheneth me."*

A new day had indeed broken. Not long after the publication of the poem, I was driven by my father into Cambridge, where I was to lodge for a year with a godly couple who kept a grocer's shop on the outskirts of the city. My further education was to consist of a year's secretarial course at the Cambridgeshire Technical College and School of Art.

Much as I loved my native village, its woods, its meadows and its quiet lanes, I left it without a backward look, and turned with eagerness toward the "far-off country."

Part Two

I shall arise and leave both friends and home
And over many lands a pilgrim go
Through alien woods and foam,
Seeking the last steep edges of the earth
When I may leap into that gulf of light
Wherein, before my narrowing Self had birth,
Part of me lived aright.

C. S. Lewis
SPIRITS IN BONDAGE

1

THE STREETS OF THE University city of Cambridge were for me "alien woods" indeed, and I loved them. I might not be an undergraduate and ride around on a bicycle with a black academic gown flowing out behind me, but nevertheless I was a "student" and, in my mind, entitled to my share of the city's mystique. To my land-lady, my studentship was completely on a par with that of any other "college girl," and since she had read my long poem in the Christian weekly before she met me, I had already earned a place of respect in her heart. To my embarrassment (and secret pride?) she treated me with considerable awe. I was a poet, a writer; she, so her attitude implied, was one of thousands who had read my "work"—and now I was to be her lodger. Little did this simple Christian woman know how she was boosting my "literary ego," which was probably already begin-ning to feel its feet a little!

She had turned their upstairs sitting room into a bed-sitter for me, but I was to eat my main meals with the family, in the little room downstairs behind the shop. It was a far cry from the spacious farmhouse and the peaceful Essex countryside. But for me, with my thirst for experience, it was just what I wanted. Upstairs by the spluttering gasfire, I wrote poetry each evening when I should have been learning my shorthand homework. My landlady tiptoed around me as if I were Christina Rossetti or Elizabeth Barrett Browning. I am sure such reverence did me nothing but harm; but to be fair to my sixteen-year-old self of the time, I was irritated rather than pleased by it.

At college I was finding out that there is a world of difference between the approach of the dedicated high school teacher, and the take-it-or-leave-it attitude of the men and women who find themselves trying to impart variable knowledge to a hotch potch of young people whose aims in life range across a field of widely different interests. The feeling of moving together toward a common purpose, shepherded firmly by those who knew where they wanted us to go, even if we didn't quite know ourselves, just did not exist anymore. For the first term I felt vaguely homesick for the genteel authority of my old school. I didn't feel too comfortable about being pointed half-heartedly into various directions, when I had grown so used to being led.

By the beginning of the second term, I had resolved to get the hang of shorthand and typing as well as I could, and to pay as little attention as possible to things like commerce and bookkeeping, which left me stone cold. There were lessons which I should have enjoyed—English and French literature, for example, were part of the course. But I could muster very little enthusiam for either, because the teachers didn't inspire me. I think I realized then that I probably would never have made the grade at university anyway. I lacked the sheer mental discipline, not to mention intellectual sharpness, which would have been essential for university studies. Yet would this have been true had I had those two years in the sixth form, training my mind along the lines to which I had already become accustomed? Who can tell. And it no longer matters, anyway.

For me, that year in Cambridge is chiefly memorable for a relationship I formed with a girl called Lesley. She was tall, fair and of rather striking appearance generally, and she aroused my curiosity, though I could not have said why. Her eyes were large, gray and heavy-lidded; her mouth was wide and soft-lipped, curling down slightly at the corners. It was the face of a dreamer. When she walked, she bent her shoulders slightly, as though to minimize her height. The result was a kind of stooping gait, and as she always moved with a measured pace, a slow glide rather than a walk, all eyes would turn on her when she crossed a room. I remember seeing her cross the main hall one day while a bunch of boys were clustered around a radiator. As they saw her approaching they turned to stare, then sang out in only slightly muted tones: "Have you ever seen a dream walking?"

One day, before I had actually spoken to her, we happened to be sitting next to one another in a bookkeeping lesson. Suddenly she turned to me, and without preamble, said: "You're a religious person, aren't you?"

I was taken aback, to say the least. Nothing I had said or done in her presence could possibly have given rise to such a challenge. I recovered my composure in time to say that if, by religious, she meant did I know God personally, then yes I did. But what had made her ask the question? She was evasive in her reply, smiled her enigmatic smile, and looked at me with her deep, dreamy-eyed gaze. "I envy you," she said.

It was the beginning of a friendship which was to have a real impact on my life. We found that we had quite a bit in common. Her first love was English literature, and like me she had been advised by her headmistress at the Perse School in Cambridge to go to a university. But her family circumstances were such that she felt it necessary to start earning a living.

I soon found that she belonged to a somewhat bohemian set, most of them undergraduates, amateur actors, artists and the like, who met of an evening in the basement of a café in King's Parade. She took me along on one occasion, but I was terrified of the sophisticated, self-assured people I met there, and cowered in a corner. Realizing her mistake, Lesley never asked me along again. Employing what I then felt to be a doubtful compliment, she told me that I was too "innocent" for such company. She also told me her friends had asked her why she bothered with such a timid, inarticulate little mouse as me!

It is true that I was still both timid and inarticulate. Although my stammer had improved a little, I suffered deeply about not being able to express myself in words. I knew that this inability had nothing to do with the stammer, since it was not just a question of being unable to get the words out. I wrote a poem at about this time in which I agonized about the fact that words were only at my command when I wrote them down, never when I spoke them. When I look at that poem today, I can still feel the anguish with which I wrote it.

But meantime, Lesley was introducing me to the Romantic school of literature. She lent me books by Oscar Wilde, and I became fascinated by his cynical paradoxes. I dabbled, at this time, in a kind of pseudo-intellectualism which was symptomatic of my ever increasing urge to probe beneath the surface of things, to see beyond the apparent horizons which bounded my spiritual experience, to discover a third dimension to the religious teachings which formed the background to my faith.

Lesley warned me dramatically that she was not good for me. She went on about my "innocence," and I wondered if she took a secret delight in this idea of having a certain amount of power over my mind. She told me that "once your feet have danced on enchanted ground, you can never be the same again." Getting a taste for it, I told her that I didn't want to be the same again. I wanted to ride on, discovering new lands, new horizons; I didn't want to stand still. She looked at me sadly from under her melancholy eyelids, and shook her head.

I believe that she had a genuine love for me—she told me so often enough, anyway, and I was certainly fond of her. She was one of those rare spirits who shine out in a crowd, and I was sad, after my marriage, to lose complete touch with her. I longed so much that she should find God, yet I sometimes wondered whether she really wanted to know him at all, or if she didn't rather enjoy belonging to that category of people who say they wish they could believe, but cannot. We talked and we walked, we argued and we reasoned, but all to no avail, as far as I could see. She would simply shake her melancholy head and sigh.

And yet for that time we spent together in Cambridge, our two lives did overlap, it seems, in a way which left its mark on each of us. For me, our friendship was to heighten my already growing fear that God, and what I loosely called "Art" could become rival loves. For her, I believe it was a time when she was made to think seriously about the claims of God upon her life; a time when she did stop to listen, however briefly and unwillingly, to the calling voice of the waters in the Spring of Life.

To sum up the dilemma in which I thought I found myself, I wrote a short story for the religious weekly which had published my poem. The story was about a girl who turns away from the call of God because she believes that her heart is already given to another, in her case Art as expressed through the medium of paint. Painting is her life. She lives for it. She feels incomplete without it. It is her master. Therefore, she cannot, she will not surrender herself to God. One day while climbing a tree in order to be "alone with her thoughts," she falls and breaks her right arm. It is crushed beyond repair, and has to be amputated. When the girl realized that her right arm, "her very life," has been taken from her she is in despair. But as in all good religious stories, good finally triumphs. In her tragedy and helplessness, she turns to God for help. He gives her back what he had taken from her, and before long she is drawing with her left arm as well as, if not better than, she did with her right.

The story was published, and I received for it the then princely sum of three guineas. It was fifteen years later before I was to write another story for the magazine—and then the payment was exactly the same! Another short poem, written at the height of my friendship with Lesley, was also published that year, this time in a secular magazine. Lesley took a sheaf of my poems to show a literary critic friend of hers, and this is the comment that came back to me:

"It is unnatural that so young a girl should have such an easy, effortless and continuous flow of words with which to express her meaning. Your poety is dangerous to you. You pour all your emotion into it and use it as a substitute for living, which should inspire your poetry, not understudy it."

Maybe he was right. If so, then what had happened to my eagerness to get on with the business of living, with my thirst for experience? A short verse written at that time shows that a certain element of disillusionment might have been creeping in:

> *The world is a dreary, conventional place*
> *Full of conventional people*
> *Doing conventional things;*
> *Life touches few of them;*
> *Love wakens some of them;*
> *Death must find them all.*

It seems that I was ready to mount my steed and gallop on to see what lay over the brow of the next hill.

2

ON THE CORNER of the street, the newspaper vendor sang out his wares: "Cambridge or London, Cambridge or London, Cambridge or London?" For me, it was a question which had nothing to do with newspapers. I must make up my mind—whether to stay on in Cambridge, or to look further afield for a job. The call of the capital now began to lure me. Cambridge, much as I loved it, did not hold the secret I was looking for. The time-weathered beauty of the ancient buildings, which had been the seats of academic learning for centuries, was not for me. This was not my promised land. But London, surely, must hold all of life's secrets; all the answers to all the questions I had yet to ask must be there somewhere, in the mysterious, hidden, teeming life of this great city which was to me still only a magic word—*London*.

The new minister of my little home chapel said if I liked he would write to the Baptist Church House in London and see if there was an opening for a young journalist with the *Baptist Times*. The reply came back—not at present there wasn't, but there was a vacancy in the accounts department of the Missionary Society, and if I cared to settle for that for the time being, I would be ready to fill any gap on the paper when it became available. My heart sank—accounts—and I hated figures. I was assured that my work would consist solely of typing. Reluctantly, I agreed to take the job. After all, it was London, and maybe I wouldn't have to wait so very long for an opening on the paper.

I lodged with the family of a previous minister of my home church, who now had a pastorate in London. I stuck the job out for six months, but when I could see that I might have to go on for ever waiting for an opportunity to use my literary flair, I gave my notice. I found the job unbearably tedious, and when I was given the chance of becoming secretary to the Secretary of a Missionary Training College for women on the outskirts of London, I readily accepted. On the face of it it seemed like jumping out of the frying pan into the fire as far as tedium and lack of opportunity for creativity was concerned. But I was so sure that this was what God wanted me to do, that I moved into my little room at the college with a willingness bordering on eagerness. My enthusiasm was dampened somewhat by finding that the room was in the annex, and had only one small window, which looked out on to the landing, so that I was dependent for fresh air on what little came in at the landing window. The view, of course, was non-existent. But the college was in a lovely setting, and I felt sure I would be happy here.

I was, up to a point. But somehow that phrase "up to a point" was beginning to figure all too frequently in my thinking. There was this growing sense of isolation, of not quite fitting in; this yearning for a fulfillment of my deeper nature which, in itself, made me feel guilty.

Christians should feel fulfilled, for Christ is fully satisfying, surely. Sometimes I felt that all I wanted was a boyfriend—someone to love, someone to love me. But when I thought about it, I knew that my need went deeper than that. For the boy would have to *understand* me; he would need to share my appreciation of the aesthetic, as well as the purely spiritual.

I looked around me and wondered if evangelical Christians ever felt as I did about these things? Maybe I was wrong, maybe I ought not to be so indulgent toward the poetic side of my nature. It was bad to be so inward looking, all the best evangelical teachers told me so. Sometimes I searched the Bible for something which would confirm my own feelings about beauty and poetry and philosophical thought. It was there in the Psalms, of course, and in Job. I was puzzled by the Song of Solomon, yet felt that there was more to this little book than met the eye. Strange, when you think about it, that theological scholars who threw up their hands in horror at the idea of any part of the Scriptures being of an allegorical nature should practically insist that this book must be a spiritualized picture of Christ and the Church, and could not possibly be meant to be taken literally. But I was not looking for flaws in the thinking of my betters, only in my own.

What I really wanted to find in the New Testament, was some consolation for my vague feelings of guilt, for my lack of fulfillment. But all I found was Paul's warning to the Colossians: "Beware lest any man spoil you through philosophy and vain deceit, after the tradition of men, after the rudiments of the world, and not after Christ. For in him dwelleth all the fulness of the Godhead bodily, *And ye are complete in him...."*

But I wasn't, was I? Had Lesley, after all, been right?

Had she lured me into enchanted woods? Had she made me drink of that cup which creates, instead of assuaging, a thirst? Was I spoiled by "philosophy and vain deceit?" I felt confused, and so very alone.

The girls at the college were kind, but aloof. Sometimes I felt they were more concerned about my spiritual growth than about me personally. This was not true of all, and I still remember with warmth one or two kind faces, and warm hands which reached out to me during this solitary period of my life. The discipline of the college was strict, even in those post-war days. The students had to keep an account of every minute of their time. When they went to the lavatory, they had to record the time spent there as "recreation." They had to take the bed covers off their beds before they knelt down to pray; and I still remember the embarrassed silence which followed during a special meeting when an active missionary, home on furlough, told how on the mission field she had found bed covers to be far easier to wash than blankets! A few of the students dared to laugh with delight, but the rest, along with the staff, wore expressions of cold disapproval at such anarchy! The students all wore navy blue uniforms with starched Eton collars, and they would stand around reading their Bibles while waiting for a meal to be served rather than be seen wasting "the Lord's time." From quite a young age, I have always had a love for color and style in clothing, and I remember feeling guiltily conspicuous in my brightly colored blouses and skirts. In a dark and sober forest of navy blue, I was the only splash of brazen color to be seen!

In the evenings, I went up to my little room, glad to be alone. One or two students who felt I needed "drawing out" had the habit of putting their heads in at my window as they passed along the landing outside my room. Much as I longed for companionship of the right kind, I felt this to be an unforgivable intrusion upon my privacy.

Along with my seriousness and my withdrawn manner went a desire to kick over the traces. How I loved it when a visiting American missionary, a young girl in her twenties, walked down the lecture hall to give her talk, causing all eyes to turn, and a shocked silence to rend the air. Was she wearing a mini-skirt, or lipstick, or *no hat*? None of these things. But, while all the sober-minded students were wearing knee-length skirts, this missionary was sporting the *New Look*. The skirt of her dress actually came down to her ankles, and in the brim of her fashionable straw hat was a bunch of red poppies! Her shoes had heels, and she smiled with an easy charm as she swept up on to the platform. Such wordly bowing to fashion, such indiscretion, such a bad example to all the would-be missionaries there! I wanted to run up on to the platform and hug her.

One day I sat at my desk by the window looking out on to beautiful lawns and the flower beds, and the blossom on the fruit trees, dazzling bright against the blue of the May sky, and I asked myself, what if God wanted me to stay here for the rest of my life. In the kitchen garden, I could see the navy blue backs of students bent over their weeding and hoeing. In my typewriter was a long list of all the missionary societies that were connected with the college, and on my desk another list of names and addresses of past students was waiting to be typed on to perforated labels, ready to stick on the college magazine which was due out that week. What if God wanted me to do this for the rest of my life? Was I willing? A feeling of panic rose in me. I couldn't; I couldn't do it. But as I sat there, I felt that the voice persisted: *But what if I asked you to?* After a long moment, I bowed my head. *If you want me to, Lord, then I will.*

Looking back, I think I meant it.

Meantime, I was encouraged by a letter from the Christian paper who had published the poem and story. I must be eighteen now, they had figured out. Could I write another poem telling of the two years that had followed the writing of *Second Daybreak*? I wished I could, but my heart felt barren and empty of poetry, somehow. I wrote and said I would do an article, but could not manage verse. They agreed, though they felt that "all those people who had been so inspired by *Second Daybreak* would have dearly loved another poem."

I had, in fact, had letters from a number of people after the poem's appearance—most of them single members of the opposite sex, for some reason! I had corresponded with some of them for a time, and have even met two of them. One was an earnest young man, a sufferer from T.B., who told me frankly that he thought the Lord might intend us for each other. I told him, that much as I liked him, I somehow didn't think so. Another, older man, a Methodist minister, wrote to tell me that he was preaching in Cambridge while I still lived there. I went to hear him preach, hoping that in his message I might detect something of that appreciation for beauty and poetry which filled my mind so much at the time. But his preaching was a little dull, and when I introduced myself to him afterwards, he was overcome with shyness. He ran after me when I had left the church, and tried to apologize for his coolness. But I couldn't think of anything to say to him either, and we parted with a polite handshake. Later he called at my digs and asked for me. He told my landlady (much to her delight!) that he wanted me to go with him to hear the madrigals sung on the river. But I was at home that weekend, and we never met again.

Now I sat down to write my article, my followup for the poem that seemed to have caused such a stir. I called it, *What do you seek?* and began by quoting a poem by Mary Webb:

> *Fair, fierce life! What will you do with me?*
> *Take me and break me,*
> *Hurt me or love me,*
> *But throne me not lonely and safely above thee*
> *Sweet Life!*

It was a cry from my own heart, of course. But I went on to point out that young people everywhere were looking for Life—abundant, satisfying life. "Whoso findeth Me, findeth Life," the Lord had said. What could be plainer? What indeed!

Following the appearance of this article, I received a letter from a Cornish poet, who, so he said, had wanted to write to me after he read *Second Daybreak*, but somehow hadn't found the courage. But now, he said, he could hold back no longer, since the things I had now written had struck such an echo in his heart.

The rest of my days at the college were now enhanced by a correspondence with this man—about fifteen years my senior—which was both stimulating and satisfying. We poured out our souls to each other, and although I knew that he far outstripped me both intellectually and artistically, yet his letters did meet a need in me, as mine, so he assured me, did for him. He was deaf, and had been practically blind from childhood. He lived with his saintly mother in a cottage in the Cornish tin mine area, and everything he wrote seemed to echo the stark isolation in which he lived.

He was later to become a distinguished writer, a modern prophet who today ranks highly among English poets. He has risen to these heights against fantastic odds because his brilliant poetic gift is coupled with a stern but deep Calvinistic faith, which makes him fairly unique among artists. I recognized this uniqueness in the first letter that he wrote me, but could not foresee, then, where my diffidently grateful reply would lead me.

3

"WHAT WOULD YOU SAY," I asked my mother, "if I told you that I was going to marry that Cornish poet I told you about?"

Though the subject had, in fact, been broached in the latest letters from Cornwall, my whole being rebelled against the idea. I couldn't. I just couldn't. He was not really for me—I felt sure of that in my heart. But as I tossed and turned in my little bed that overlooked the landing, I argued with myself that this is just what I had said when I felt God might want me to spend the rest of my days at the Missionary Training College. I had said, *Yes, Lord I will*, then. Was he not asking me to say it again? Hadn't I begged not to be left "icily, numbly asunder" from warm, pulsating Life? Was this not a challenge to face the seemingly impossible with God, to fulfill a mission which maybe he had been preparing me for all these years? This man longed for love and companionship and understanding, if possible, even more than I did. He was asking me if I would be that companion, that lover. What if he was blind and deaf, almost gray, and fifteen years older than me? What did that have to do with love? But

87

my heart cried out, *No, No, not that, Lord. Please, not that!*

My poor mother said: "If you marry him, don't expect me to come to the wedding. And Dad says that if you do, he's finished with you for good."

I stared openmouthed. "But if I feel it's what God wants me to do?"

"I've told you. I want to hear no more about it."

I confided in a friend of the family to whom I felt I could talk, a Methodist lay preacher.

"My dear, you mustn't do this thing. It's wrong, wrong, wrong for you. You're much too young to know what you're doing. He isn't for you. He's eccentric—and from his letters I'd say he's egocentric, too. You'd be terribly unhappy. Why must you always think God wants you to do the hard thing? You must write and finish the affair at once. Don't even agree to meet him. Finish it."

I could see that he was right. Relief mingled with the vague feeling of having missed a chance to come to grips with "far, fierce Life" again. My thirst for experience was becoming almost a greed. What had I really known of life during the past three years since I left school? The only real life I had lived was within myself. Yet I knew they were right—my mother and the mature friend who now expressed his concern for me so fiercely.

I wrote and told my poet friend that I felt our correspondence should end. He was expecting of me more than I was ready to give. He was angry. He wrote me a bitter letter, saying that I had been swayed by "lesser minds"—people who knew nothing of what we had shared. He even threatened to include a paragraph in his next book in which he would reveal to the world how fickle I had been!

I knew, then, that I had done the right thing. God had

once again put me to the test, a "sacrifice of Isaac" type of test. I could only hope that he looked down with approval on the results of the testing. At any rate, the whole episode matured me as probably nothing else could have done.

And I certainly needed maturing. As I look back on these teenage years, I realize that in spite of my intensity of nature (or perhaps because of it) I had developed in a very erratic and inadequate way since leaving school. I had been too much on my own, had cut myself off from the guidance of older people before I was ready to go it alone. I was paddling my own canoe before I had bothered to learn anything about the rudiments of canoeing.

Sexually, I was certainly immature, almost innocent. I knew nothing at all of this aspect of human love, and did not really want to. Platonic love was my ideal. I could see no connection whatever between the physical and the spiritual. My Cornish poet friend had tried to introduce me to the meaning of erotic love, and it was partly this element in his letters which had repelled me. I wasn't ready for that yet.

Intellectually I was immature, and I knew that the pseudo-intellectualism of the Cambridge days had done me no good at all. I needed the discipline of guided study. Lesley had presented me with concepts that I was mentally unfit to grapple with. I was like a non-drinker being given spirits before I had even tasted beer. The result was very much the same. The fact that my parents could not help made matters worse. I remember my mother weeping because she felt I had become a stranger to her. My high-flown talk, which I must have practiced on her, lacking the courage to practice it on anyone else, frightened her. We had always been so close, and now she was out of her depth. The fact that both my parents were obviously hopelessly out of their depth where most of my ideas were concerned gave me a false sense of my own intellectual superiority. I cannot say I like the teenager I am writing about very much, but she must be presented, as she is part of the finished picture.

Spiritually, I think I was more mature than many of my contemporaries. Christ was my all in all. The more I became aware of my own inadequacies, and the more I suffered inwardly over my state of confusion, and over my sense of isolation, the more I needed to turn to him, and the more I clung to him. Over all was an unshakable trust in him, in his sovereignty in my life, in truth of his Word, and the assurance of my own salvation. Salvation was most certainly for me a well from which I regularly drew water; but did I draw it with joy? Or was this part of the promise yet to be fulfilled? From this particular vantage point I find it difficult to say.

It may well be said that, in the light of what I had just written, then I certainly made a mistake to cut off my education before it was complete, to cut myself adrift from the guidance of superior minds. And in one sense I am ready to admit that to do so *was* a mistake. I do not ever remember saying to the Lord at that time: *Lord, show me what to do. Do you want me to go to university or not? I only want to do your will.* I was to pray this prayer many times in later life, as has already been shown, but I do not remember praying it at sixteen. I only remember an overriding desire to get out into the world and start living. Did I take a wrong turning there? Or can we ever do this if we believe in his sovereignty? It's a question I have often asked.

At any rate, after the Cornish poet affair, I recognized that I was once more at a turning point. The experiences of the past three years had raised so many doubts in my mind; a vague desire to go back and start again made me look into the possibility of doing an external university course. I had had my taste of city life, and now an urge to go into retreat, to come to terms with myself again, made me think that a spell at home in the country might be just what I needed. Once more I asked God to make the way plain, and after receiving an encouraging letter from Wolsey Hall, Oxford, I packed my bags once more and said good-bye to the Missionary Training College.

My poor parents, relieved no doubt, that I managed to extricate myself from my emotional entanglements, did all they could to encourage me. Maybe my mother felt it would be a good thing to have me under her maternal eye again. My father bought me a desk, and they installed it in the large end room, which had once been the country retreat of the London family in pre-war days. My mother lit a fire in there everyday, and I settled down to delve into the doubtful delights of Marlowe and Alexander Pope. A poem written at this time shows a little of what I felt at the outset:

> *Softly open the door.*
> *High walls, wide windows,*
> *Fire's first red roar*
> *Warming soft shadows. And by the chimney there*
> *Six rows of books, a lamp, a table and a chair.*
> *A flame leaps in the chillness of my soul.*
> *Ah, here is refuge. Refuge from the world;*
> *From eyes that search, and hands that move*
> *And voices, voices, interminable voices....*

4

GOD HAD UNDOUBTEDLY led me home to my country haven again, but not for the purpose of giving me a university degree. Not long after Christmas, when I had completed only one term of my studies, my mother was taken ill. Sylvia was away at this time, but she came home to help me look after the invalid.

There followed a happy domestic period, for my mother's illness was not serious, though she did spend a few weeks in the hospital because the doctor just could not understand why her temperature wouldn't go down. The mystery was never solved, but her illness certainly became one of the "all things that work together for good to those who love him."

Sylvia and I decided to arrange a series of "squashes," as they were then called, in the farmhouse. Our aim was to reach the young people of the village with the gospel, and we started by inviting along the nucleus who already belonged to the chapel. These were encouraged to bring their friends, and we promised to provide not only a speaker, but a soloist and a personal testimony. There would also be plenty to eat and drink.

At the big table in the farmhouse kitchen we worked away making flapjacks, gingerbread and anything else we could find in our mother's recipe book. We made sausage rolls and cheese straws, mince pies and short bread, and we counted and recounted in a frantic attempt to assess whether our supply was going to meet the demand of the forty or fifty young people who had promised to come.

We had invited as our speaker the evangelist who had brought his tent to the village five years previously, and who, with his wife, had become quite a friend of the family in the intervening years. He said that he would be glad to come, and might he bring along a young man to give his testimony? We said, "Fine, fine," and then he added that the young man he had in mind lived in Saffron Walden, our nearest market town; that he was actually an artist, "quite an interesting sort of chap."

I tried hard not to let my curiosity about this evangelical artist, this "interesting chap" take precedence in my mind over my own evangelical zeal, which had first led to the arranging of the squash. It is true to say that I had never yet actually met a conservative evangelical of either sex who had any interest in the arts, so perhaps my curiosity was excusable on that ground alone.

When the evangelist and his wife arrived, they had the young man with them in their car. As he came into the house, my first reaction was one of surprise. Although he was, in fact, only in his late twenties, he looked much older. Dark-haired, and wearing horn-rimmed spectacles, he had the closed-in look of a recluse. As I made small talk with him, I thought to myself:

"Who could ever reach him? Who could ever break through that shell of defense he puts up against the world and set the man inside free?"

The question repeated itself in my mind as he gave his testimony. I don't remember what he said. I only remember the tension he seemed to create in me. In spite of his forbidding countenance, it was a gentle face, vulnerable as a child's. It was the face of a man who had suffered. To my own question, "Who could ever reach him?" the answer was already forming in my mind: "I could, Lord, if that's what you want me to do."

In between my studies, I was at this time working on an allegory which expressed the conflict I felt where Christianity and aesthetics were concerned. Some time after that first meeting, I sent the manuscript off to Saffron Walden, accompanied by a short letter asking Arthur if he would give me his opinion of what I had written. Addressing him formally as Mr. Mitson, I told him that I knew of no one else who was qualified to judge the manuscript from both an artistic and an evangelical point of view. I was not quite prepared for the result—a reply covering nine closely written sides of foolscap. It was all I could have hoped for, and more, for over and beyond the comments he made about my writing, was the evidence of what I really wanted to know above all: here at last was a "kindred spirit."

"It has been said," he wrote, "that intellectual knowledge tells us about the world. It gives us knowledge *about* things, not knowledge *of* them. It does not reveal the world as it is. Only emotional knowledge can do that."

I had never heard anyone speak of "emotional knowledge" before. In my letter to him I had said that I could not describe myself as a rational thinker, and that any knowledge that was mine was the "fruit of experiences of the soul." I had added that I had no confidence in my own intellectual ability to judge the literary value of what I had written, and would be grateful if he would do so for

me. That he should take up my point about emotional
versus rational thinking, was more than I had hoped for.

"This capacity for emotional experience," he went on,
"is not necessarily found in 'educated' man. Many are as
barren as their uneducated brethen. Why is this? One
reason is that modern education is founded upon science, and not upon art. The child, so we are told, is
educated for life, and life to the majority, is closely bound
up with money. The fact that the child is an individual
with a distinct personality matters little. Educating his
sensibility, his awareness of values, has no place in the
curriculum, hence the poverty of aesthetic experience.
You, I think, will agree with this. How many people of
your acquaintance, whether Christians or not, can appreciate any of the arts? I don't mean a technical appreciation, but an emotional one. If your experience is anything like mine, there are very few. This being so, the
number of evangelicals who have this capacity is nar-
rowed almost to extinction."

This was a new viewpoint, as far as I was concerned. I
thought of Miss Beaumont and Mrs. Appleby, who, no
doubt quite unconsciously had educated my awareness
of beauty and true values, and thought their kind might
well be a dying race. Arthur went on to tell me that he
sometimes felt almost ashamed to say that he painted,
and considered painting as a vital part of his life, because
he knew that many people, especially his evangelical
friends, would regard him with suspicion.

"Yet the artistic temperament," he wrote, is much
more conscious of the eternal; not a physical consciousness, but a thought consciousness. After all, we do *think*:
emotionally think. So few Christians do that. You are the
first Christian I have met who is well acquainted with
poetry. Philosophus, the hero of your allegory, desires

completeness. This comes very near my own desire: probably it is another way of saying it. My longing is for fulfillment—to be, in essence, one with Christ."

So he knew it too—that longing for completeness, for oneness with God himself, a yearning to:

> leap into that gulf of light,
> Wherein, before my narrowing self had birth,
> Part of me lived aright..."

Didn't all evangelicals believe this, then? Wasn't "reconciliation" the key word on the lips of all the teachers and preachers that I knew? Wasn't salvation a turning to Christ for cleansing from sin, and did not his death on the cross reconcile us to God? Of course! But there was more—much more for which they rarely found words. John 3:16 had been preached on countless times, but how often did they preach on John 17:3? "And this is life eternal, that they might know thee, the only true God, and Jesus Christ whom thou hast sent." *This is life eternal*—the same life eternal that every man has as soon as he believes. *To know God.* How simple, and yet how profound: the most basic need of the human soul....

Probably neither Arthur nor I would have identified our longings in quite those terms at the time we first met. But I knew that when he said his longing for fulfillment was to be, in essence, one with Christ, here was a man who spoke my language.

"To have found God," says Tozer, "and still to pursue him is the soul's paradox of love, scorned indeed by the too easily satisfied religionist, but justified in happy experience by the children of the burning heart...."

Arthur and I both knew ourselves to be "children of the burning heart." We burned to "know God"—to know him, as I was to find out later, not as a friend knows a friend, but as a man knows a woman in a love relationship.

I read and re-read the pages of Arthur's letter, hardly daring to believe that this man, who shared so many of my deepest feelings and ideas, should live only a few miles from my home—was in fact, born and brought up there. Although I was still only nineteen, I had begun to think that I would never meet anyone—let alone a man —who spoke my own language. But God had brought his answer to my prayer right to my very doorstep.

We began to correspond, and from here our relationship developed and flowered. Once or twice Arthur came to preach at the chapel, and we entertained him for the day. We talked, we walked; but our relationship remained for awhile on a strictly intellectual level. Neither of us had ever found it easy to relate to others on a personal basis, and Arthur, especially, found the transition from an academic level to an emotional one very difficult. But one day the breakthrough came, and he telephoned to make our very first "date." As I put down the receiver and went to tell my mother, I was walking on cloud nine.

But although our courtship proper began from this time, we both had a lot of ground to cover before we were ready to share our lives together in the comprehensive relationship of marriage. We began to open up our hearts to one another now, as well as our minds. I told Arthur all about the time I spent at the college, and the mental and spiritual conflict I had undergone there. He shared with me his similar experiences when he was catapulted, at the age of nineteen, into the army. Those years had left a scar on his mind which might never be fully eradicated. The marks of suffering I saw on his face on that first meeting dated back to the trauma of those war years.

In one of his letters he quoted this passage from John MacMurray:

"But in practice, sensitiveness hurts. It is not possible to develop the capacity to see beauty without developing also the capacity to see ugliness, for they are the same capacity. The capacity for joy is also the capacity for pain. We soon find that any increase in our sensitiveness to what is lovely in the world increases also our capacity for being hurt. That is the dilemma in which life has placed us. We must choose between a life which is thin and narrow, uncreative and mechanical, with the assurance that even though it is not very exciting it will not be intolerably painful; and a life in which the increase in fulness of creativeness brings a vast amount of delight, but also of pain and hurt."

After this quotation, Arthur had written: "Do you agree?"

Did I agree? I might have written the words myself, so close were they to my own heart. In a later letter he said:

"I have found one poem that perfectly expresses the army in all its ramifications. It concludes:

> There is no island on this island
> Shut in, depressed before the flow
> Of youth that wears a color
> Sere, as they too will grow.

My heart went out to him, and I told him that in an odd way I found an echo of this in my own experience at the Missionary Training College—though, of course, the two institutions were poles apart! It was the *uniformity* which I found so deadening. It was completely different from the recognized expedient of school uniform, which I had rather enjoyed at high school: it was a uniformity that went deeper than the navy blue serge dresses and white Eton collars. I had felt that there was a uniformity of thought and outlook, of personality, even, which went completely against my nature, and I felt partially destroyed by it. So I understood only too well the far greater damage which Arthur had experienced during those war years. Upon his sensitive spirit the wounds had gone far deeper, and the resulting scars were more severe than the outside world could guess. I sensed, in the early stages of our relationship, that there would be periods of depression and darkness which would need all the patience and understanding that I could give. It was one thing to share deeply in these things of the heart, and quite another to relate to each other as ordinary flesh and blood human beings. An extract from one of Arthur's letters to me at this time shows something of the difficulties we faced:

"It is strange, although not strange, that your letters come just when my mind is prepared to receive them. I thought I could come to you, and love you, alone, but God has had to show me that he must give me even this. Because I couldn't always see, faith has failed, sometimes to reach out into the unknown. I am amazed at your perfect understanding. You have found me in the dark tunnel into which I had been driven; but at present I'm blinded by the light which you have shown me.

"There has been something inevitable about our relationship. I knew, eventually, I should come to you, but I despaired of ever finding you. I used to think of you, but when I attempted by some plan to reach out to you, I despaired. When I came, I was driven by longing, and in the longing, I had lost my difficulties. The longing, in the will of God, brought me to you, but my difficulties returned with greater force because I had committed myself. It was here that you reached out to me with your loving understanding. I do need you to show me the light, and, as your have already said, to comfort me.

"The hours in the wood will always be sacred to us; or would it be better to say 'the hours in eternity'? I have often thought that we must have said things to each other that no human being has ever said before. I give you my love in the presence of God."

5

WE WERE MARRIED, the following year, on my twenty-first birthday, at the village chapel overlooking the green where I had played so often as a child. As the words *"Till death do us part"* were spoken, Arthur enclosed my hand in a grip which promised a lifetime of deep love and devotion. The chapel was crowded, but we were alone. Which of the large congregation who so lustily joined in the singing of the last hymn could possibly have guessed why we had chosen it?

> *Bright skies will soon be o'er me*
> *Where the dark clouds have been....*

To them we were a young couple who had not yet tasted life. What did we know about dark clouds? When we sang "My Savior Has My Treasure," we each referred instinctively to the gift of love He had given us—our love for each other which would last into eternity. We were to sing that hymn years later on a very different occasion, when the private significance of those lines was to change dramatically. But for the present, our love, the deep and certain knowledge of having been literally

103

"made for each other" was the bright blue of our sky and shining promise of our future.

After a honeymoon in Devon, we began our married life in a little terraced house in Saffron Walden. Our front door opened straight on to the pavement, our back door led into a narrow garden, and the only lavatory our new home boasted was outside, but we were happy and secure in the blissful experience of making a life together. As we stood and surveyed our little sitting room with its books, its pictures and its handmade pottery, we looked into each other's eyes and said: "Now, at last, we can be *ourselves*."

But not quite in the way that we had imagined, for even while we spoke the words, I was already pregnant! I vomited my way through the next few weeks, and was not very good company for Arthur when he came home from his studio for meals. I lost weight rapidly, and could think of little else than the problem of nourishing my unborn child.

I suppose even in those days some couples used to sit down before their wedding day and discuss such vital issues as how many children they would like, and when to start a family; but we never had. When I hear or read of men who confess that one of the chief reasons for marrying was that they wanted children, or women who talk about "security" and "making a home," I am puzzled, because none of these things seemed to have entered into our thinking at all! We married because we loved each other and felt incomplete without each other. It was as simple as that. Perhaps this is true of most other people, too. But if so, why can't they say so? All the other things, the fringe benefits of marriage, surely follow out of this.

I often think about that version of the marriage service

which says that marriage was first ordained so that the "natural instincts" might be directed aright, was secondly for the procreation of children, and was thirdly for the "mutual help and sustenance" that the one might have for the other. When I go to a wedding where this particular form of service is used, my whole being cries out in protest, and the rest of the ceremony is spoilt for me: for surely it should be the other way round? God gave Eve to Adam because he was incomplete without her: the natural instincts and the children followed automatically out of their union of love, not the other way round. I sometimes wonder what kind of men sat down and wrote that marriage service!

At any rate, no one was more surprised or delighted than I was when I found myself pregnant. I had never thought what it would be like to have a child of my own. Now, however, I began to think with great excitement and longing about having Arthur's child. Would it look like him? Would it be fair like me, or dark like Arthur? I thought it would be rather nice to have a little dark-haired boy with a Mitson's nose.

I had a little fair-haired girl with a Funston's nose. I looked into the cradle and thought: "A girl. Poor little soul. She'll have to go through all *this*!"

Like pregnancy, childbirth had taken me by surprise. I knew, up to a point, what to expect, but nothing can really prepare a girl, who, two or three years previously may have been sitting at a school desk, for the shock of this experience. I remember feeling that it must be a punishment for something. But for what? For the sin of Eve? For being a woman? It was my first taste of a bewilderment which was to recur over the years.

But I set myself to the task of motherhood with a will, and with enjoyment. I was thrilled with my tiny daughter, and proudly displayed her to Arthur when he bent tenderly over me in the hospital bed. We took her to stay for a few days on the farm, and while Arthur painted, my mother and I took the baby for country walks. Once when we were about a mile from home, the baby began to cry inconsolably, and my mother suggested sensibly that the best thing to do was to feed her. We sat in a corn field in the warm summer's sun, and I gave my baby the breast. A contentment spread through the three of us as my mother and I sat shoulder to shoulder against the sweet smelling, ripe corn, with the pungent earth and the prickly stubble underneath us, and the serenity of a June sky over our heads. It was one of those timeless moments when the whole of nature seemed to be in tune.

But the bewilderment of finding myself to be a woman was not confined to the physical. Arthur belonged, in those days, to the Christian Brethren, and although I was happy with the group of warm-hearted folk who met each week at the Gospel Hall in Saffron Walden, it came as something of a shock to find myself classified (not verbally, but by implication) as a second-class pilgrim by reason of my sex. Now I have no doubt that all good Brethren will earnestly protest that I must have misunderstood the teaching of their assemblies; or worse still, that I understood only too well that this was the teaching of the New Testament, and rebelled against it!

But this is not the case. I accept the belief that God has ordained men to be the teachers and leaders in the church, but as with any spiritual truth or principle, this concept is wide open to abuse by those anxious to obey the letter of the law. Coming as I did from a church whose teachings were also biblical, I was struck by the heavy emphasis which was laid by the Brethren on this

one aspect of Paul's teaching. At home, in the village
chapel I had led a mixed Bible class because I happened
to be the one best suited for the task. I was well grounded
in a knowledge of the Bible, and presumably the minister
and deacons felt that my Christian witness and experience fitted me for this bit of service. But I realized that
according to Brethren thinking I should have been replaced by *any* male, no matter how unsuitable. At the
week-night prayer meeting at chapel, I prayed because
Christ was real to me, and because the needs of the world
were heavy on my heart, but I have never, to this day,
found it easy to pray in public. I had taken various parts
in chapel services for special occasions and had spoken at
midweek meetings when asked to, though it always cost
me a great deal to do so. None of these things had come
under the heading of teaching, and in no way had I
usurped the God-given authority of any man. I accepted
the biblical teaching on these things as naturally as I did
any other truth.

But here at the Gospel Hall the whole subject of
women in worship was thrown into stark relief by the
rigidity of the Brethren's rules. No woman ever prayed in
the prayer meeting, was not allowed to open her mouth
in a Bible study discussion, could not even choose a
hymn, could not even share a thought. Lady missionaries could give a talk to other ladies, but no male
must come within a yard of the room while she was
uttering! Anxious to bring myself in line with biblical
teachings, I tried hard to accept my new position in the
fold. Not that I wanted to do the things I was excluded
from doing. It was, in fact, a great relief not to be expected to pray in public anymore: I no longer had to do
battle with my inbred nervousness and my fear of other
people. It was the implication that lay behind the rules

which affected me so deeply. Try as I would, I could not help feeling depressed and rejected by it all. For the first time in my life, I began to feel that I had somehow had the misfortune to be born into the world as a member of the inferior sex. The role of woman, which up till now I had joyfully acclaimed as mine, now seemed downgraded, undesirable; as though I had turned over a prized possession and found the word "sub-standard" stamped on it in indelible ink.

Brooding on these things in the early days of my marriage, I remember saying to Arthur one night in bed, in a strangled voice:

"I didn't ask to be made a woman!"

To which he replied gently. "And sweetheart, I didn't ask to be made a man."

Somehow, I didn't find that much of a comfort at the time!

The Brethren, of course, have become much more open about these things in recent years, though many of them do not understand how deeply the "stigma" has affected their women over the years, and have been heard to express surprise that the ladies still do not make themselves heard in the prayer meeting, even though they are now free to do so!

I have to record that the seven years I spent with them, though they had rich and happy moments, did little to help me develop into a natural, full-flowered womanhood. As with my father's verbal violence, the extreme, unnatural emphasis which the Brethren put on the matter of the subjection of women was, all unbeknown to me, forging a scar on the back of my mind which would take many years to heal.

Meanwhile, our second daughter was born. As with most parents awaiting the birth of a second child, we had hoped for a boy, since we had a girl already. But when I saw her pointed chin, wide eyes and little turned-up nose, the matter of her sex became entirely irrelevant: she was just like her Daddy, and my joy was complete. We called her Frances.

6

UP TO THE TIME when we needed the third bedroom for the children, we had made it into a kind of den. Here I would lie on an old settee and read, while Arthur painted. He was at this time moving toward a more abstract form of art, and it delighted me to see how a new freedom was developing in his creativeness. He had said in one of his early letters to me that he would probably never amount to much as an artist because he was too subjective. "An artist must have a personal image," he said. "And I have a very poor imagination."

There may have been a measure of truth in what he said, but when we returned from our honeymoon, he brought with him lasting memories of the lovely old harbor at Brixham, in Devon. He had made some sketches, and now he began to work on them imaginatively, allowing his brush the kind of freedom that he perhaps had not quite known before. Few people understand why painters produce abstract works of art. They expect a picture to look as near as possible like an exact replica of the subject the artist has worked from. They have misunderstood the secret of the artist's creativity, the drive which lies behind the making of music, poetry, sculpture, painting. . . .

Arthur once wrote: "Whatever is said in creative work can only be a shadow of the substance within the artist. He cannot communicate himself."

This, of course, is true. But the creative drive which is at the heart of him makes him go on trying, albeit unconsiously. It follows from this that the artist, whatever his particular medium for expression may be, will sometimes produce something which seems complex, even incomprehensible, to the onlooker. For the substance within the artist is made up of so many different elements, most of which are received through the senses. The artist, therefore, expressed his sensibility, in all its complexity.

A painter who recently spoke about his work on a British television program spoke of the "beautiful freedom" of abstract composition. "How can you possibly portray on paper or canvas what you see in a harbor?" he asked. "If you just draw boats lying side by side in the water, you will only have presented one simple facet of what you are receiving through your senses. The sounds, the smells, the movements, the fluidity of it all; the shapes of the boats and the sails and masts, always moving, but never in the same direction, the changing light, the poetry of the colors. Only an abstract form can hope to capture any of it."

I am only quoting from memory, but I thought at once of Arthur's abstract harbor scenes; the beauty of line and form, the harmony, the "poetry of color," as the artist so delicately expressed it. Some of these paintings are still hanging on our walls, and are among my favorites. In those early years, several of Arthur's pictures were hung in London galleries. The little den at the top of the house proved to be a refuge from the more routine activity of the bread-and-butter work he did all day, lettering and signs.

It was not long, of course, before the creative bug bit me again too. While I was carrying the children, I was happy in the all-absorbing natural process of creativity. I dreamed and planned for my unborn babies, as all mothers do. I sewed pretty smocks for myself and little dresses for the babies, and I walked out into the country, absorbing the sights and scents and sounds in the firm conviction that the child growing inside me would receive what I took in through my senses in much the same way as it would receive nourishment from what I ate!

With Elizabeth in the pram later, I would walk under the trees in the park, talking to her about what I saw, telling her what beauty lay around and pointing out how lovely was the tracery of branches and leaves overhead. I thrilled to all the tender possibilities of motherhood, to the precious responsibilities of creating and molding and nurturing human lives and minds. These children were ours, Arthur's and mine, made in our image. Yet first and foremost they were God's, given by him, entrusted to us, and first and foremost they were made in *his* image.

When they were both little, my evenings were free. With the two of them safely tucked up in their beds, I settled down to write. I had decided to begin a novel, and with a great sense of adventure and excitement I launched out on a wide open sea.

It has been said that the effort of every true poet is to unify his experience. I suppose this is true of the painter, the musician and the sculptor too, up to a point; it is perhaps more certainly true of a certain kind of novelist. My friends said, "Are you going to write a story which will spell out the gospel message for those who have

never heard it?" Or at least, that was the gist of their
enquiry. I replied that I intended to write about life as I
knew it. They nodded doubtfully.

When I look now at the allegories I wrote when I was
nineteen, the work that played such an important part in
bringing Arthur and me together, I am impressed, and a
little saddened, by their freshness. The sadness arises
out of a lurking suspicion that some of that early freshness of vision and style may have been lost over the years
in my attempt to write what evangelical readers would
appreciate. For I soon found that no general publisher
would take on work where the evangelical faith showed
through too clearly, nor would any evangelical publisher
consider fiction which did not follow the pattern set out
for it over the past fifty years.

"The final problem," says Virginia Ramey Mollenkott,
"artistic freedom, is and always has been a sensitive one.
The evangelical public, alas, too often desires a book
which will not disturb its preconceived notion. In matters both of doctrine and of behavior, the evangelical
author soon feels pressure to abandon his own insights
and to conform to the existing pattern. The Christian
public thus demands that its authors "lie" in the interests
of Christianity, either by pretending that all is happy and
simple when all is *not* happy or simple, or by conforming
against their better judgment to certain rigid norms. But
Christ, who is truth, needs no falsifying to save his face."

All this I was to discover later, the hard way. As a
young wife and mother, writing away in the evenings at
my novel, I was blissfully unaware of the heartaches
which awaited me in my literary career. I wrote that first
novel in longhand—all ninety thousand words of it. As
the characters unfolded under my pen, continually taking me by surprise, and as the plot developed, growing

out of the characters, I felt happy and fulfilled: a perfectly
"rounded" person at last.

At the other end of the dining room table where I
wrote, Arthur worked away at a correspondence course,
for his eyes were now set on a difference goal, theological
college.

7

SOMEONE HAS DESCRIBED the call of God as being "not the emotion of a moment, but the trend of a lifetime." This is how Arthur felt when he said to me one day, out of the blue:

"What would you say if I told you that I believe God was calling me into the Baptist ministry?"

I told him that I would not feel in the least surprised. For although Arthur had never mentioned to me before the leanings he had in this direction, yet when he told me of it, I felt a calm acceptance, as though I had been already prepared for it. That Arthur would ever leave the Brethren had never occurred to me, nor had I ever wished that I might leave them. Where Arthur belonged, there I belonged too.

Looking back, I think it must have been at about this time that Arthur began to paint fewer and fewer pictures. There were several reasons for this apart from the fact that all his free time was absorbed in study. In one of his letters to me he had said:

"When a man is regenerated, he becomes a unified being. The change is radical and complete. Conversion has been defined as the process, gradual or sudden, by which the self, hitherto divided, consciously wrong and unhappy, becomes unified and happy through its acceptance of divine realities. The converted man now has a God consciousness, a realization that in him dwells God by the Holy Spirit. His old nature, the nature of sin, has been crucified with Christ, and now he lives the life of the Spirit.

"We know this to be real, not only by experience, but on the authority of the Word of God. 'If any man be in Christ, he is a new creature.' Now supposing this redeemed man, prior to his conversion, was a poet or an artist; does it not follow that this peculiar capacity died with his old nature? Not at all. Much of his previous subject matter may have, but he is still essentially a poet, and as such will have a poet's apprehension of eternity. No doubt it will be fed and developed by the Holy Spirit through the Word of God, but he is still an individual with his own particular gift.

"This, of course, does not necessarily mean he will continue to write poetry or paint, as the case may be. I think you get an instance of this in Oswald Chambers, who is in many ways unique among evangelical Christians. Before his conversion—and after, I think, for a time—he hoped to become an artist. In the accepted sense he did not realize his early ambition, but was supremely an artist for God. His vision, and the expression of his vision, was that of an artist; in consequence, it was powerful because of its individuality. I suppose we—that is, you and I—could be classed as the seers, the mystics, whose awareness of the eternal is emotional."

In some ways, I see a parallel between Arthur and the man of whom he wrote, Oswald Chambers. For fifteen years or more following his call to the ministry, Arthur's output of pictures was minimal, though he did do some sketching on vacations from time to time. Yet in his new, God-given calling, his vision, and the expression of that vision, came through his preaching. As with Oswald Chambers, the vision has been that of an artist, and consequently his preaching is powerful because of its individuality. He is a prophet in the strict sense of the word.

Sometimes when people try to put into words the feeling they have about Arthur's preaching, to say why it touches them where many other kinds of preaching do not, I want to explain to them it is because he is essentially an *artist*: a seer, a mystic, whose awareness of the eternal is emotional. For obvious reasons I say nothing of the kind. I just smile and say: "I think he's marvelous too."

All was not plain sailing. Several years were to elapse before Arthur could begin his college training, and we were certainly to find that we needed patience, that after we had done the will of God we might "receive the promise"!

One difficulty was that even though Arthur passed the necessary exams, the Education Authority refused to make him a grant. For science they might have done, but for theology, no. But we were unswerving in our conviction that God had called us, so we were not dismayed. There was only one alternative. We sold our home and Arthur's carefully built-up business, so that we could finance a college course, and the four of us moved into two rooms in a friend's house on the outskirts of London. There was a tiny dining room, and one large bedroom, which we divided into two with curtains. In one half went our double bed, and in the other half the children's two little beds.

In spite of our cramped conditions, the first year was a happy one. We lived out of suitcases and boxes stored under the bed; there was even a sack of potatoes behind the bedroom door, the only space we could find for them. Elizabeth went off to the local school, and Arthur set off every day for college, leaving Frances and me to fill the days as best we could. In spite of the spirit of adventure with which we had embarked on the move, the second year in the flat was not always easy. I began to long for my own home again, and would walk around the streets looking at other people's front doors, just longing to be able to let myself in at my *own* front door and close it behind me.

When Arthur began to "preach with a view," I would put Frances in a pushchair and set off to find the manse belonging to the Church where Arthur was due that Sunday, if it were in the London area that is. If the manse were empty, I would snoop around looking eagerly into the windows. Would this be our new home? My heart would beat with excitement as I began to set the rooms out in my imagination. I would think of our furniture, still in store at Saffron Walden, and would begin to make plans for new covers and curtains.

Once I took a train to Canvey Island, a small shanty town on the Essex coast, divided from the mainland by a narrow creek. It was a glorious day, and both the girls went with me. We spent the morning on the beach, and the children revelled in the golden sand and the open spaces. After the noise of the city, it was paradise to us all. When we had eaten our picnic lunch, we set off across the fields to look for the manse: for Arthur was to preach at the Baptist Church that Sunday. The house was empty, and it was detached. The town might leave much to be desired, but this could make us a lovely home —and there was the sea, always there, just across the fields.

"Are we going to live here, Mummy?" chorused the girls. "Is this house going to be ours?"

"We have to wait and see. . . ."

"Wait and see what?"

"To see if God wants Daddy to be minister of this church or not."

"I hope he does want him to," said Frances eagerly, "because then I could play on the beach *every day.*"

A settlement was slow in coming, and the friends who had talked about "a big step to take" and "burning your boats behind you" began to shake their heads in an I-told-you-so fashion. Our home was gone, and our business, and so, almost was our money. Yet, strong in our faith, sure that God had a purpose in all the waiting, and grateful to him that our material needs were constantly being provided for in unexpected ways, we pressed on doggedly.

There was one weekend when Arthur and I both touched a low. He was doing a holiday job at the time, and I came in to find him scanning the newspaper Situations Vacant column.

"But you've got a holiday job," I said.

"It isn't a holiday job I'm looking for," he said in a small, strained voice. That night the demon doubt assailed me.

I remember standing in church that Sunday to sing the hymn the minister had just announced: "Begone Unbelief." As I sang, the words seemed to stand out in my mind, emblazoned there with such brightness that I had to hold on to the pew in front:

"And can He have taught me
To trust in His Name
And thus far have brought me
To put me to shame?"

Arthur was out preaching that day, but when he returned, I told him how God had met with me and spoken
to me through the words of the hymn. Hand in hand we
gave thanks to God for his unfailing, unchanging love. It
was surely a privilege to have our faith tested like that.
The call would come, and we must be ready.

When the call did come, it was midsummer. Our first
church was to be in the heart of the Sussex countryside,
in the beautiful village of Lindfield. Both church and
house were small, but to us they were everything we
could desire. After the restrictions and the trials of those
last weeks in London, our hearts were bursting with joy
and praise. Arthur took up his new pastoral duties with
eagerness, the children ran wild in the countryside, and I
began to think about writing again.

Just as in the early days of my marriage I fitted my
writing into the evenings so that my days could be given
wholeheartedly to my home and my children, so now I
set aside time in the mornings, while the girls were in
school. The afternoons were usually taken up with
duties in the church and neighborhood. I have always
found that, rather than tending to make me neglect my
other duties, my writing has more often served to make
me more diligent in other respects! Determining that
nothing else should be made to suffer, I usually attack
other jobs with a special measure of vigor while I am
actually engaged on writing a book. I get through
housework at great speed, put that little bit extra into my
culinary efforts, attack church work with a will, give

conscious attention to the needs of the family, and generally go out of my way *not* to do that thing which would be so very easy to do: that is, to become totally absorbed in the business of creation to the exclusion of all else.

At Lindfield, when I began to write children's books, I involved my own children as much as possible in the whole process, reading them my day's work each evening before they went to bed, and encouraging them to offer suggestions or criticism. They never did actually criticize, and their obvious interest and absorption in the story was a source of considerable encouragement to me. If the tale held their attention, then I reckoned it would hold the interest of other children too.

Both our daughters were beautiful in their own way. Both were fair, but while Elizabeth's beauty was of a more classical, almost Grecian kind, Frankie's was an elfish prettiness made up of dimpled cheeks, sparkling blue eyes, a turned up nose and a ready smile. In a sense, their looks corresponded to their personalities. Elizabeth was always the more reserved of the two, complex in character, not easy to get close to. Frankie, on the other hand, was open, straightforward and easygoing. And, as with my sister and I when we were children, Frankie was the demonstrative one, while Elizabeth tended to hide her feelings.

I remember one incident which shows their contrasting personalities rather well. They had both saved up their pocket money to buy me a birthday present, and happened to say to a certain generous widower in our church that they were going into the village to buy the present on a certain day. To their embarrassment, he insisted on going with them. When they came home, both girls scuttled upstairs to hide the present, but after a while they appeared in the kitchen where I was baking, with odd expressions on their faces.

"Everything O .K .?" I asked breezily.

They exchanged a funny look.

Then Elizabeth blurted out: "Mummy, he wouldn't let us pay any of it!"

"He told us to keep the money for ourselves," put in Frances, (rather gleefully, I thought!) "Or spend it on sweets."

"And did you?" I asked.

Elizabeth shook her head. "No, we know we're not allowed to buy sweets until we've asked you. But that's not the point..."

All at once, her lip trembled, and she burst into tears.

"I don't want the money!" she burst out. "I wanted to spend it all on you! I've been saving it specially, I don't want it!"

It took all my tact and wisdom to explain to that generous widower that he must take his money back. Though I did not put it in so many words, I tried to convey to him how my daughter's desire to give had been spoiled for her, and how confused she felt as a result.

But I knew that Frances—my dimpled, cuddly Frankie —was not in the least troubled about the incident. She was already mentally spending the unexpected bonus!

8

IN ORDER TO OUTLINE the development of my writing career, I need to go back to the early years of my marriage. That first novel, of course, had never seen the light of day. When it was finished, I had been completely carried away by my sense of achievement. I couldn't believe that *all that* had come out of me! I have learned since that most writers feel like that when they have written their first book, and that some go on feeling like it every time they write a new one. To me, the whole experience was exhilarating, beyond anything I had yet tasted in the field of creativity, and I was sure I had written a bestseller.

I attended a writers' conference at about this time, and I took my precious manuscript with me in the bottom of my suitcase. There were one or two publishers taking part, and at the end of the conference, I took my courage in both hands and approached the one who seemed most likely to be interested. Very haltingly, and with great embarrassment, I confessed that I had a manuscript which I hoped he might look at. I half expected him to back away, but instead he showed genuine interest.

"Let me have it, let me have it," he said genially. "After all, that's what I'm here for. We publishers are looking for new writers all the time. For all I know, you may be another Elizabeth Goudge!"

I might indeed! The idea went to my head. At home I talked in enraptured tones of my weekend at the conference, telling Arthur of all the interesting people I had met, of the pleasure I had found in talking of nothing but writing for a whole weekend. And then I handed him my prize plum: *a publisher had actually carried off my manuscript to London and was going to consider it.*

A month later, I saw the red mail-van stop outside our door, and then heard the postman's knock. My heart sank. The shape of the parcel he handed me was all too familiar. I wanted to push it back into his hand and tell him to take it back where it came from. I have often thought since that writers must be just about the only people who open the door to the parcel postman with a look of hostility on their faces! Inside the parcel was a letter saying that although the publisher had found my novel interesting and colorful, he very much regretted that he could not accept it for publication by his firm. The book, so my genial conference speaker assured me, was in fact a "near miss" as far as they were concerned, and it might well be that some other publisher would feel prepared to take it on.

It took me several weeks to get over this bitter disappointment. All that work, all that devotion to the task, evening after evening for months and months; and then all the rewriting and the final typing of the manuscript. Ninety thousand words of inspired fiction—*rejected!* No subsequent disappointments, and there have been plenty, could quite compare with the bitterness of that initial blow. In vain might friends say, "Try another publisher; all writers have to do that! The first one you try hardly ever takes it!" What did they know about it? How could they enter into my sense of *personal* rejection?

A few years previously, in a rash moment, I had sent my allegories to C. S. Lewis for an opinion, and he had taken the trouble to write me a personal letter. He said that he had to resolutely refuse to look at any such manuscripts, because he just did not have the time, but that he could tell me right away that the only way to get work published was to try one publisher after another. He himself had gone for years without getting any of his work published! Now, in my bitter disappointment, I didn't want to be reminded of that letter. I wanted to succeed *now*—not ten or twenty years later!

But as always, Arthur was there to encourage and cheer, and before very long I had embarked on another story—this time a children's novel. There was a children's fiction competition being run by a religious publisher, and when Arthur said, "Why not enter?" I thought, "Why not?"

I can't remember what happened to the adult novel. I must have sent it around to other publishers, but if so I have forgotten what they said. I do recall that the one other publisher whom I had met at the conference and come to know fairly well since, read it and asked me to come up to London and talk to him about it. He and a colleague did all they could to encourage me with my writing, and I shall always be grateful to them for that. But no one wanted to publish my novel.

When I had finished writing the children's story, I sent it up to the competition judges. A few weeks later I received a letter saying that my story had been short-listed. The prize-winners' names were to be announced in mid-December, and those concerned would be asked

to go up to London to receive their prizes at a public
ceremony. By early December, the suspense was becoming unbearable. I had received no other communication
from London, but neither had my manuscript been returned. What had happened? Could it be that I had won
a prize? In my imagination I saw myself going up on to
the platform to get my prize; saw the brightly colored,
hardbound book which would subsequently appear on
the shelves of bookshops all over the country—bearing
my name, and the title of *my* book.

Only a week to go before Christmas, and still no news.
I could bear it no longer. I rang up the organizers of the
competition and asked if they could give me any infor-
mation. They were *so* sorry ... my manuscript should
have been returned to me last week. It had been the very
last one to be eliminated, and it was touch and go till the
last minute whether it was going to be among the
prize-winners...

As I put down the phone, the call box seemed to sway
around me. I couldn't believe it. Another *near miss*. It
would have been easier, I felt, to have had the manuscript back in the beginning, never to have had that letter
about being short-listed. It was like having the prize
dangled in front of your eyes and then snatched away
just as you raised your hand to take it. *Why, Lord, why?* I
cried.

But as Job discovered, when you cry out to the Lord
like this, there is no way he can give you an answer
straight away. He has to spell it out slowly, sometimes
over a period of years. And at that particular moment in
my life I knew the only thing to do was to pick myself up
again, brush myself down, and start all over afresh. I
sent the manuscript around to all the publishers of religious fiction I could think of, but to no avail. With one I

made the unpardonable error of saying: "This story was a near miss in the Christian Fiction Competition arranged by so-and-so." The manuscript came back with a snooty reply: "This story is not up to our required standard!"

Several years later, the same publisher accepted that story without question, asking simply that a few details might be brought up to date... The reason? They had, the previous year, accepted a story from me which they liked very much, and had obviously forgotten, when the rejected manuscript arrived on their doorstep, that they had read and rejected it some seven years earlier! Suddenly a book that was "not up to our standard" became a publishable proposition! Between the writing of that story and its publication some thirteen years had elapsed.

The book which started things rolling for me was the one I wrote at Lindfield. No subsequent pleasures in the field of writing can quite compare with the thrill I felt when I held in my hands that very first published book. I could thank God, then, even for all the years of waiting and for the bitter disappointments I had suffered. And perhaps in time the thing I most desired would come to pass, and I would go on to write a publishable adult novel.

The position of pastor's wife provided me with plenty of material for fiction writing. Before long I was bursting with ideas. The only problem was finding time to get down to the serious business of writing. The children were growing up. Elizabeth was eleven, Frances nine, and, apart from all that had to be done in the home and church, I was still doing quite a lot of public speaking. But I tried to set aside a certain amount of time each day while the girls were at school to work on a new novel. As it proceeded, I knew it was the best thing I had written. And I felt, too, that I had at last managed to strike a happy medium between what evangelicals wanted to read, and what I was determined to write!

"The trouble with your writing is that it falls between two stools," my London publisher friend told me. This was to remain a problem for longer than I guessed. Practically all the books I have written have had to be rewritten, sometimes twice over, to suit a publisher's requirements. But for the time being, I was happily absorbed in my writing, savoring once more that "rounded" feeling of being fulfilled in every part of me.

"My writing *matters* to me," I told myself one day on a wave of jubilation. "I couldn't live without it now."

The novel was rejected. And rejected again. And again. Then it fell into the hands of a magazine editor who came to live near us. Full of enthusiasm, he rang me up—could I go over and talk to him about my story? He liked it very much indeed and would like to serialize it in his magazine. I was full of misgiving. His praise and enthusiasm for the story had somehow come too late to cheer me after the disappointment of having failed with it as a book. I wasn't sure that I wanted my novel messed about with to make a serial story for a religious weekly. I knew it would have to be altered to suit the taste of the readers of that particular magazine, and I was right. In fact, one third of the story had to be cut, and the plot tailored accordingly before I eventually agreed to sign a contract.

The story came out with a splash of headlines announcing it as a "powerful new serial by a gifted writer." I was invited to a reception in a London hotel, where I met other writers and artists connected with the magazine. I was introduced to one and another as "the

author of *All Loves Excelling*," and praise and admiration
seemed to come from every side. I was swept off my feet
by it all, and yet at the back of my mind was the thought:
"This isn't really what I wanted at all. This isn't where I
wanted to be...."

The payment for the story was the best I had ever had,
and what is more, there was something else to go with it.
The editor wanted me to write them two serial stories
each year. Carried away by the prospect of writing fiction
which people actually wanted to read, and for which
there was an editor just waiting to say, "Thank you very
much!" I signed the contract.

It was not the prospect of financial reward which made
me accept the editor's offer, poor though we were at the
time. In fact, I remember thinking with misgiving: "We
shan't be hard up any more—and I don't think I shall like
the idea of that very much. Things will never be the same
again. I shall no longer *need* to make all my own clothes,
or the children's, and the thrill and satisfaction of feeling
we can get by on a shoe string will have gone." We had
proved over and over again the truth of the promise that
if we put first the kingdom of God and his righteousness,
all these things would be added, and I enjoyed living
along those lines. Then I began to wonder if this might
not be a way of "all these things," or at least some of
them, coming our way. It would be great to be able to
take the children to the sea for a holiday. We might be
able to buy a car, even, after a time, or at least buy decent
presents for each other at Christmas and birthdays.

But my doubts about having some extra income were
all for nothing. The next story I wrote under the terms of
the contract did not suit the taste of the new editor, and
unless I was prepared to make drastic changes in the
plot, he would not accept it. Appalled that I should have

gone to all that trouble to write a story specially for the magazine, only to find that, in spite of the contract, I was back in the position of being rejected, I opted out of the agreement. I knew I could not go on like that—turning out stories to suit a magazine editor who was obviously not really in sympathy with my literary aims. The whole thing was a waste of time.

I began to think about writing a serious novel for book publication again. I had read an article in the *Reader's Digest* about a child who had died from leukemia, and I was appalled by the pathos of the story. I found myself toying with the idea of writing a fictional story about a Christian family who underwent a similar trial, depicting the triumph of faith in the midst of overwhelming odds. I saved the article for future reference.

What was to follow has been told at some length in my book *Beyond the Shadows* and consequently I do not intend to go into any detail here. Suffice it to say that even while I was reading that magazine article, grieving inwardly about the agony of the child's mother, and filing the story away with the idea of using it as a basis for a novel—at the very same time, my own Frankie, my lovable, exuberant nine-year-old, had the seeds of the same dread disease in her body.

Eighteen months later she would be dead.

Part Three

Here on the mountain I have spoken to you clearly: I will not often do so down in Narnia. Here on the mountain, the air is clear, and your mind is clear; as you drop down into Narnia, the air will thicken. Take great care that it does not confuse your mind. And the signs which you have learned here will not look at all as you expect them to look, when you meet them there. That is why it is so important to know them by heart, and pay no attention to appearances. Remember the signs and believe the signs. Nothing else matters.

C. S. Lewis
THE SILVER CHAIR

1

"IT IS OUT OF the pain and rejection, and the dread of being forsaken, that some of the most creative energies come," says Tom Houston. "It is out of that travail that men are really born again. Lose the idea that the new birth is something that happens once for all when you are converted. Being made a new creature in Christ Jesus will go on as long as you are in the probation of this life. Periods of trial bring to birth some new thing in you that God desires. Isaiah speaks about the "treasures of darkness." In context it means literal treasures that are hidden in dark places, but it is a suggestive phrase. There are some treasures that come to us out of darkness that cannot come to us any other way."

Out of the dark period during which our precious daughter suffered and eventually died, so many treasures were to come. But not all came immediately. Some have had to be mined, painstakingly and painfully, over the intervening years. Those who have read the story will know something of the treasures which came out of the actual experience at the time, for, in a measure, they will have shared those enrichments with us.

135

It was shortly after Frankie's death that I sat down to write the story. I wrote it down because I could not contain it. The desire to share the experience was a secondary thing. I have told in that book of the events which led up to her illness, but for the sake of those who may not have the opportunity to read it, I will outline them here.

I wrote in the previous chapters that even while I was planning to write a fictional story about a family who had tragedy to face, the identical tragedy had already begun to take place in my own family. But there was something more, too, because I was at this time turning over in my mind the whole complex question of suffering and pain.

A family up the road from us had lost a twelve-year-old boy, suddenly, with asthma. One minute he was in the kitchen helping himself to a piece of cheese; the next minute he was dead. He was one of our Sunday school scholars, and when I met his mother in the High Street some time later I could not think of anything to say to her.

News of missionaries who had suffered and died for their faith, stories of Christians behind the iron curtain who were imprisoned and tortured for naming the name of Christ made me curl up inside with horror. What if it was me? I couldn't even contemplate such a nightmarish possibility.

Then trouble struck even nearer home. A Christian friend of ours lost her husband suddenly and was left with two young sons. In the lives of this bereaved family I saw the kind of triumph over tragedy that I had known all along should be possible, but had never been able to imagine happening for me.

"Perhaps," I wrote in *Beyond the Shadows*, "my resolve to write a story about a family who had this tragedy to face, was, in fact, my personal way of working this thing out for myself. Perhaps I thought that out of my own creative resources the answer would come. I do not know."

Instead, the answer came out of bitter personal experience. Yet how can I say "bitter" of an experience which was, in so many ways, the most enriching thing that ever happened to me? We are brought back once more to this paradox which is at the very heart of all things: to find your life, you must lose it; to know what joy is, you must suffer; to gain eternal life, you must die to self. Yet the cry of the poet Francis Thompson is the cry of the sufferer down the ages: *Must all Your harvest fields be dunged with rotten death?*

There is no answer to be found anywhere upon earth to the question of why innocent children suffer—except that it is one of the laws of a universe inhabited by a fallen race that the innocent suffer with the guilty. For things to be otherwise, man would need to be other than he is: a fallen creature with the freedom to initiate good or evil.

The memory of Frankie crying out in despair: "Why doesn't Jesus heal me, like he did the sick people when he was here on earth?" is overlaid with another memory. We had just arrived home after one of the gruelling visits to the hospital for treatment. As we waved the hospital service car off, Frankie looked up at me with shining eyes: "You know, Mummy, all the way along in the car, some words kept singing themselves in my mind: *Because Jesus died for me, he will take care of me all the time.*" Commenting on this incident, I wrote:

"The cross of Christ must be central to all our thinking. Unless this is so, there is much in life that we shall fail to understand, much that will entirely defeat us. For it is only through his atoning work on the cross that any of his blessings can be ours. *Because Jesus died for me*—this is the key without which we cannot enter in. To a little sick girl of ten he gave the key."

It was through suffering—his own suffering—that God chose to redeem us from our fallen state. He became the suffering servant that we might become heirs of his kingdom. Our minds stagger at the mystery of it all. C. S. Lewis says in *The Problem of Pain* that "in self-giving ... we touch a rhythm not only of all creation, but of all being. For the eternal word also gives himself in sacrifice, and that not only on Calvary...."

I often think of Jesus weeping by the grave of Lazarus. Why did he weep? He knew that all power was given unto him in heaven and on earth, that in a matter of minutes he was going to call forth the dead man from the grave and demonstrate his forthcoming victory over death. Yet as he looked on the weeping people he groaned within himself and was troubled: he bowed his head and wept. Why? Because he was, in that moment, one with the suffering of humankind. His heart was heavy with the agony of being human—an agony he had chosen to bear. Here we see God giving himself not only in death, but in life. We can never do more than dimly guess at the cost to God of becoming man. Who but Christ, who was God incarnate, could tell us that no sparrow falls to the ground without the Father's "participating presence," (as the Greek implies)? And if he is in the suffering of the fallen sparrow, how much more is he in the suffering of his children who are of more value than many sparrows?

This is one side of the picture. The other side is the one that we are sometimes slow to understand. For suffering is also bound up with God's love for us—a love which is so great, so unlike human love, that we find it incomprehensible. "Behold," says John, "what manner of love (love as from another country) the father has bestowed upon us, that we should be called the children of God!"

As usual, C. S. Lewis has phrased it more tellingly than I can ever hope to: "When Christianity says that God loves man, it means that God *loves* man: not that he has some 'disinterested,' meaning really indifferent, concern for our welfare, but that, in awful and surprising truth, we are the objects of his love. You asked for a loving God: you have one. Not a senile benevolence that drowsily wishes you to be happy in your own way, not the cold philanthropy of a conscientious magistrate, nor the care of a host who feels responsible for the comfort of his guests, but the consuming fire himself, the Love that made the worlds, persistent as the artist's love for his work, and despotic as a man's love for a dog, provident and venerable as a father's love for a child, jealous, inexorable, exacting as love between the sexes. . . . The problem of reconciling human suffering with the existence of a God who loves, is only insoluble so long as we attach a trivial meaning to the word 'love,' and look on things as though man were the center of them."

But as Arthur and I agonized over the prospect of losing the child given to us by God ten years previously, the child we had loved and cared for, nurtured and cherished, the child who was part of ourselves, the incarnation, as it were, of our love, it was not easy to see our suffering—let alone hers—in terms of God's love for us. Yet through it all there came to us the deep assurance of an all-pervading, comprehensive love in which we were safely enclosed, even in times of deepest darkness. Out of this assurance grew a joy inexpressible, a peace past understanding. For we recognized at the last that there is *nothing*—absolutely nothing that can separate us from the love of God which is in Christ Jesus our Lord.

These fruits of the spirit provided an answer to my own personal heart-searchings about how it was that Christians could pass through deep and terrible waters without being overwhelmed, as God had promised. I saw, now, that it is the indwelling spirit of God himself who causes us to triumph at such times; that he himself carries and bears us, as on eagles' wings.

We begged for healing for our child—"claimed it," in fact with unswerving faith, but finally found ourselves echoing the words of Paul: "For this one thing I besought the Lord thrice, that it might depart from me. And he said unto me, my grace is sufficient for thee; for my strength is made perfect in weakness. Most gladly therefore will I rather glory in my infirmities that the power of Christ may rest upon me. Therefore I take pleasure in infirmities, in reproaches, in necessities, in persecutions, in distresses, for Christ's sake: for when I am weak, then am I strong."

Once more, the answer was contained in paradox.

2

OUR AGONY WAS naturally heightened by the practical problems which always accompany such a situation as ours. Elizabeth was twelve, Frances almost ten by the time we realized there was to be no miracle. Not that we ever stopped believing God could do it: we simply began to feel that it was not in his perfect purpose for us. But how to protect our children from this knowledge? We resolved that life should go on as nearly normally as possible that nothing in our behavior or our attitudes should betray our secret knowledge or the hidden grief in our hearts.

The supernatural joy God gave us at this time is impossible to communicate to others: we trusted we were communicating it to our children as well as to those around us. We prayed together as a family each morning, we talked together, we went out together. We were determined that life should be as full and satisfying as we could possibly make it. We answered all the children's queries about Frankie's illness as honestly as we could, and though we never named the disease, neither did we pretend that there was a cure for the condition. We

141

explained how the treatment worked, and the one question we dreaded they might ask—"Will the treatment do any good?"—never came.

But one thing troubled us. We could not tell how Elizabeth really felt about it all. Being a naturally reserved child, she gave little away. There were times when we felt she must guess the seriousness of her sister's condition, but if so, she gave no sign of it. We ourselves tried to treat Frankie as we normally did, or as any parent would treat an ordinary sick child, and Elizabeth seemed to be doing the same. But there was something in her manner which vaguely disturbed us. As the end drew near, we felt sure Elizabeth must be aware of what was happening. She was almost thirteen now, and we knew that the time for pretence had come to an end.

I remember standing in the kitchen and calling her out to me, the agony of what I had to say tearing at my heart.

"Elizabeth, I know you must realize Frankie is very ill indeed."

She kept her eyes away from me, pressing the handle of a spoon into the draining board.

"Look, we thought you might like to stay with Chris and Jean for a few nights. . . ."

"All right then." Still she didn't move.

"Look, dear . . . you do realize that when you come back Frankie won't be here." I could hardly get the words out. "She'll be . . . in heaven. . . ."

Instinctively I took a step nearer the rigid form by the draining board. If only she would say something . . . or better still, burst into tears so that we could sob in each other's arms. My heart was bursting with a grief that was somehow doubled by Elizabeth's complete implacability. I longed to comfort her, but she showed no sign of needing comfort. I could not—would not accept that this was so.

"Then I'm best out of the way," she said at last.

I took another step nearer, but her whole bearing seemed to say, *Don't touch me....*

She turned and walked out of the kitchen, and I locked myself in the bathroom to cry my heart out. *This is more than I can bear, Lord; more than I can bear.*

But even while we are saying that we cannot bear it, we know that we must and shall bear it. There is a way to the other side of our agony, though it be hidden from our view. We continue to go through the motions of living and find to our surprise that we are still capable of boiling a kettle to make tea, or of changing the sheets....

I stand in the room where Frankie is lying on a sofa by the window. Outside, a bird is making frantic diving motions toward the window, tapping its beak sharply on the glass with each swoop. I remain there for a moment, transfixed by the strange quality of the scene: the dying, golden-haired child, *my baby*, and the bright-eyed urgency of the bird.

Frankie turns toward me and opens her blue eyes: "Either open the window and let it in, Mummy. Or make it go away. It's beginning to get on my nerves." Her voice is weak, a little slurred.

"Let me take you to bed, darling. You're so tired, and you won't hear the bird up there. It won't go away until it's ready—birds are like that."

But no sooner have I tucked her up in bed, than the bird appears at the upstairs window. Not the front window, which is directly above the one it had been previously worrying at, but a little side window near Frankie's bed. Once more its beak begins to tap out a message with frantic rhythm on the glass.

Frankie turns her head toward the window. "What's it trying to say to me?"

Into my mind come some words of T. S. Eliot from the *Four Quartets*:

> *Go, go, go, said the bird: human kind*
> *Cannot bear very much reality.*

Later, as I stand in the darkened bedroom and listen to Frankie's labored breathing, more words drone like a Greek chorus somewhere in the back of my mind:

> *The agony in the curtained bedroom*
> *Whether of birth or of dying.*

Her birth and *her* dying. They were too close, too close.... Oh, God, why? What is it all about? Birth and death, the body's pain and the heart's agony? Little comfort, in that moment, to know that:

> *Love is the unfamiliar Name*
> *Behind the hands that wove*
> *The intolerable shirt of flame*
> *Which human power cannot remove.*

We stand, Arthur and I, a few days later, and look down on the still, dead form of our daughter. But now, all despair, all grief, all anguish is dissolved into the sure and certain knowledge, which comes to each of us as we stand with hands clasped, that we are in the presence of the eternal. It is as though God draws back the curtain of heaven and beckons us to approach the threshold. Death is swallowed up in victory, tears wiped away by a nail-pierced hand; we see a land of perfection, of flawless joy; a land vibrant with a kind of life that makes earth seem like a living death. All is suffused with a golden light: joy, beauty, adoration, wonder—and in the center of all things, the One who is the source and spring of eternal life. And *she* is a part of it all, she whose beautiful shell lies here before us. She is free, she is whole, she is running and leaping. She is alive for evermore.

Such times of revelation come to us but rarely, for, as Eliot said, human kind cannot bear very much reality. For days we walked on a plane which seemed to cut us off from the rest of mankind. We saw them watching, but as from a great distance. We knew we should have to return to them eventually, but for the time being we were out of their reach.

We chose the same hymn that we had had for our wedding to sing at the funeral service, but now the words of the last verse took on a new significance:

> *My Saviour has my treasure*
> *And He will walk with me.*

There, on the mountain, He had spoken to us clearly—words we shall never forget. But below, the valley was waiting.

Downstairs, in the sitting room, by the sofa where she had lain, were her books, her knitting and her toy monkey. Upstairs by her bed, her slippers lay where she had last kicked them off. I looked at the two beds standing side by side, and I said to Elizabeth gently:

"Would you like us to take her bed out? Or shall we leave it for when you have friends to stay?"

"It doesn't matter."

"You understand now, don't you, darling, why we had to spend so much time with her, why we had to hide the real truth from you? Or perhaps you guessed, all along, how serious it was? We tried so hard not to let you feel neglected. You understand now, don't you? And if you've missed out on anything at all during this past year, we'll be able to make it up to you now." But she turned her face away without a word.

When people asked us afterwards how Elizabeth fared during our period of trial, we found it difficult to answer them. We could only say that we felt God had kept her apart from, yet at the same time, part of, the situation; that although she could not possibly have understood, at thirteen, what was happening in the hearts of her parents, yet with her innate sensitivity, her intelligent perception, she was able to accept, and to become part of, an experience of divine proportions. But as to her own emotional reaction to the whole traumatic experience—of this she gave no sign. Life went on. She went back to school, absorbed herself, as she had done before her sister's death, with her own friends, spending most of her time at a local farm where there were ponies to be groomed and exercised.

Life went on for Arthur and me, too. But none of us would ever be the same again. The ploughing, the harrowing, the planting, may have seemed to be the same for each of us. But for each of us there was to be a different kind of harvest.

3

FRANCES DIED IN MAY. By the end of June I had begun to write the whole story down, and by the autumn I had the manuscript ready to submit to a publisher. It was eighty thousand words long, and in its pages I had poured out my very soul. When the manuscript was returned to me a month later with a sympathetic but polite letter of rejection, I just couldn't believe it. The next publisher I offered it to said that he would like to publish it, but that I would have to cut it by one third. Though I was reluctant to do this, I felt that he was probably right when he said that I had put in too much detail, and I settled down to do the grueling work with a heavy heart.

In a sense the initial writing had been a kind of therapy. I needed to write it. But to go over the material again, cutting, rewriting and reshaping was painful drudgery. The publisher who asked me to do this then kept me waiting for a year while he decided whether my revised script was to his satisfaction, and at the end of the year—on New Year's Eve to be exact!—he telephoned me to say that he had changed his mind about the whole

147

thing. The story, he had decided, was too harrowing.

The third publisher I approached said that he was impressed with the story, but felt that it would not have a wide enough appeal to make it a viable proposition for them. My fourth attempt brought forth an encouraging reply. This firm said they would like to publish—but could I cut the story down a little more? So once more I sat down to work on the manuscript.

When eventually the book appeared, three years had elapsed since I first began to write it; three years in which I seemed to relive, over and over again, the ordeal through which we had passed. I found it difficult to understand why God was allowing this to happen. Wasn't the ordeal itself enough? Must I continue to suffer loss? Was I being punished for something? I felt bruised and bewildered.

But when the day came at last for the publication of my book, all the travail of the past years was forgotten. The book was an immediate success. All the doubts expressed by the various publishers about the story being too harrowing, not having a wide enough appeal, not giving a positive enough message of hope, were proved to be entirely groundless. From all over the world came messages of appreciation and gratitude. I was overwhelmed by what was happening. The story of Frankie had touched a spring in thousands of hearts and spoken to many different kinds of need. I felt that my personal suffering could count as nothing beside the staggering balance of pure blessing which had come to so many.

My own spoken and written ministry was enriched as a result of it all, and apart from the many letters I wrote, invitations to speak on "The Problem of Suffering" came from far and wide. Before long the demands being made on my spiritual resources as well as my time were considerable. I never ceased to wonder, and have not to this day, at the way in which God was working out his purposes, bringing triumph out of tragedy, gain out of loss, new life out of death. It was the familiar principle at work all over again.

I am brought back again and again to that saying about it being the "effort of every true poet to unify his experience." This was certainly true of all the poetry and fiction I ever wrote; it was most certainly true of *Beyond the Shadows* and *The Innermost Room*; and it is equally true of this book. And yet, I ask myself, is it possible to "unify" one's experience in this way? Am I, in fact, succeeding? Am I somehow managing to distill from the complex pattern of what lies behind me that essence of truth which makes sense of it all? And what, as Pilate so wistfully asked, is truth?

It has been said that truth is not a plain tale, and it cannot be told simply, as if it were in a straight line, with a beginning and an end, word for word, once for all. Truth is complex, subtle, manifold and often self-contradictory. I become more and more aware of this as I continue to try and capture the elusive truth that runs through my own experience and present it to any who cares to receive it. The sculptor works in stone to do the same thing, the painter in paint, but the writer must use words. And words have a habit of conveying too precise a meaning. In a narrative of this kind, they leave little room for abstraction.

When all has been said, there is only one true unifier of human experience, and that is the Holy Spirit of truth himself. He alone leads us into all truth. When we remember that the very purpose of God in sending his Son to be our Saviour was to unify us in himself, then we realize that any part of our lives which does not serve this purpose is so much wood, hay and stubble. "That they may be *one*," prayed Jesus in the garden, "even as we (Christ and God) are one." "This is eternal life, that they might know Thee, the only true God, and Jesus Christ whom Thou hast sent."

God's love will stop at nothing; so much does he desire to bring us into a relationship of oneness with himself, that he will go to any length to do it. And we shrink from such a love as this. The union between husband and wife is described in the Bible as making them "one flesh"; and Paul compares this union with Christ's love for his bride, the church. This kind of love is in the shape of a cross, and Christ died to make this union possible. He gave himself. In return, we must die to self in order to fulfill our part of the union. Here we have a mystery, says Paul. This all-embracing, all-consuming, unifying love is the love of God for mankind: his love for the individual soul.

I see this as the unifying element in my total experience; and metaphorically I take off my shoes to say it, for this is holy ground: I see God, giving himself in his exquisite graciousness, to make himself known to me in a love relationship.

And did I shrink from such a jealous love? Did I hold myself back from it, "lest having him, I might have nought beside?" Or did I sometimes draw so much satisfaction from the gifts that he had given me, from the simple fulfillment of "being used," that I forgot to draw water from the wells of salvation? I had always suffered from a basic sense of inadequacy, of self-doubt, and in times of need I would reach for my poet's pen (figuratively, if not literally) rather as a baby reaches for his comforter, or his cuddle-blanket, thinking "At least I have this. . . ."

Yet I was still consciously dependent on God for every

bit of service I did. My natural nervousness and my innate reluctance to give voice to any of the thoughts and feelings of my heart saw to that. Nor had I in any way shifted my position in regard to the doctrines I hold dear, nor slackened in my personal devotion to Christ. On the surface, everything was as it had always been.

But underneath there was a growing longing for something more; a gradual awareness of a dryness which I could not quite define. There were times when I could have cried with David: "As the hart panteth after the water brooks, so panteth my soul after Thee, O God. My soul thirsteth for God, for the living God." I searched my heart to see if I could find some point at which I was not right with God; I asked him to cleanse me of all known sin, and to deal with anything in which I might be unconsciously failing him. When I addressed meetings, and folk pressed in on me afterwards to express gratitude for what I had said or—as happened nearly everywhere I went—for what I had written in *Beyond the Shadows*, I felt humbled and ashamed, thinking: "If only they knew how dry I feel, how joyless."

I even began to wonder if what I really needed was the much talked of "Baptism of the Holy Spirit." Arthur and I had had many talks together about this, talks which usually ended in his expressing grave doubts about the whole charismatic movement, and my saying that I felt we should keep an open mind about it. It was the one thing we didn't quite agree on, though we never actually argued about it. In my travels, I had seen some whose lives had obviously been transformed by some kind of spiritual awakening; but Arthur and I had both seen those who claimed to have had the Baptism of the Holy Spirit, yet who had become hard and critical of others, sometimes saying quite scathing things about those who questioned the charismatic "manifestations." In these people the fruits of the Spirit were patently lacking. It was all very confusing.

I remember traveling by long distance coach to a Midland town where I was due to speak to a Bible Study group arranged by the local parish church, and I had taken to read on the journey Pat Boone's *A New Song*. It was the first book I had read of its kind, and when I read of how Pat's life and that of his whole family had been infused with new life, through the Holy Spirit's "baptism," my heart cried out again for the living water of God's blessing. But, I reminded myself, here was a man who had really allowed sin to overtake him, step by subtle step, until he had recognized himself to be a Christian in name only. Perhaps he had never been a truly born again Christian until that time when he was brought to the very end of himself and surrendered to the Holy Spirit's control. Yet the very phrase "step by subtle step" niggled at my mind, and I felt I had stumbled on some hidden clue to the confusion of my own mind.

Confusion? I certainly was not conscious, at the time, of any confusion. But looking back, I see that it must have been there. I addressed my meeting, feeling more nervous than usual, because of the presence of men there. (I did not often speak at mixed meetings, and the unfamiliarity of seeing attentive male faces always threw me!) But afterwards, the usual expressions of appreciation were forthcoming, and I returned home feeling tired but happy. Yet I knew it was only a superficial happiness. Underneath lay a deep discontent.

4

IT IS AT THIS POINT in my narrative that words seem to be the wrong medium for expressing what must now be expressed, and I almost wish I could switch to paint or music. Or, since words are all I have, maybe poetry would have been better. The trouble with prose, as I have already suggested, is that it forces one to be precise and literal where one would rather be abstract and obscure. Perhaps, in any case, there are some areas of experience where artistic expression of any kind fails. Certainly this is how I feel about what is to follow. I feel that I am attempting to express the inexpressible.

It was a Saturday morning. An ordinary Saturday morning in late October. I sat up in bed, as I usually did each morning, to have my time of prayer and quiet before starting the day. Someone had given me a small booklet entitled *Four Spiritual Laws*. As I looked through the booklet I began to find my thoughts centered very specifically on the question of the lordship of Christ in the life of the Christian. I put aside my books and Bible, and leaned my head back on the pillow with my eyes closed.

"Lord," I prayed, "is it possible that I haven't really understood the meaning of your lordship in my life? Can that be the reason for the way I feel? Because Lord, if that is so, then I want to know. And I *want* you to be supreme, Lord. I want *you*, and only you. . . . Take all the things I do for you . . . all my writing, my public speaking, my counseling, my letter writing, all my *doing*, Lord, and give me, instead, only *yourself*. . . ."

As I prayed this prayer, a strange sensation began to spiral within me; whether in the region of my body, or my head, I cannot say, because the very word "sensation" does not fit anyway. It just happens to be the best the English language, or any other language, can do. The "sensation" frightened yet thrilled me because I recognized it to be something completely outside ordinary human experience. Something which could not be interpreted in human phraseology. It "cut off" my prayer in mid-sentence, and replaced my fumbling attempt to express my heart's surrender with an authoritative command to get out of bed and get down on my knees. As I knelt down by my bed, the spiraling "current" inside me grew and multiplied until it suffused my whole body and mind with an unbearable ecstasy, an unspeakable joy; if there were an English word to describe a feeling compounded of terror and rapture, then that is what came upon me. I deliberately do not say "that is what I felt," because the verb "to feel" just will not do.

I was caught up in a consuming Presence which ravished me with divine love. At the same time I found it impossible to maintain my kneeling posture by the bed, because I felt myself being drawn down, down, by an overwhelming sense of utter worthlessness. As I sank lower and yet lower, my limbs seemed to become boneless, and I slid from the edge of the bed to the floor. Here I lay motionless, my heart pounding in my ears, and love, love, love was everywhere. I was shot through, consumed by burning Love.

As soon as I was in a position to entertain cogent thought, I knew that I wanted this to last forever. I could not bear to tear myself away from such an embrace. I could hear Arthur moving about downstairs, and I knew that he would soon be expecting me to appear. The thought that he might come upstairs to look for me, and find me prostrate upon the floor spurred me to movement, but my next thought was, "How shall I tell him? Will he know anyway?" I dare not look in the mirror, because I was convinced I should see a stranger there. My eyes felt bright and wild with the glory they had beheld. When eventually, having dressed as quickly as I could, I turned to the mirror to comb my hair, I saw, to my surprise, that I looked as I always did. Upon my face that Holy Thing which had come upon me had left no trace.

Arthur was reading the newspaper. He looked up as I came into the room and began to read aloud something out of the paper which he thought remarkable enough for comment. At first I was afraid to speak in case my voice betrayed me, but after a bit I mumbled a reply and went to make some coffee. As I went through the usual routine of boiling water and scalding the coffee, I felt that time was being suspended: that this was only an interval: that I had, by the necessity of everyday circumstances, been forced to interrupt a divine encounter. Yet the words "interrupt" and "interval" are words which belong to time:the encounter was outside time. So there was no sense of urgency. Only of eager anticipation.

As soon as Arthur had gone up to his study, I threw myself once more face downward on the dining room carpet. I reached out my arms toward my Beloved and murmured words which I have long since forgotten. In any case, they were timeless words, not meant to be remembered, and certainly not recorded. Once more there came the sense of consuming love, and of my own utter worthlessness.

I have no idea how long I lay there. As I have said, such moments are, in any case, outside time. But after a while I remember crawling up on my knees to lean against the armchair. Kneeling there, I started to pray for Arthur, so conscious was I that I had, for the first time in our life together, experienced something I could not share with him in any sense.

"Lord, visit my darling, now in his study. Let him, now, this moment, know your love as I have known it. He is so much more worthy than I am, of such a visitation. Oh, Lord..."

But it was as though a gentle hand were placed over my mouth. *This thing is between Me and you. Now for the present, it concerns no one else. Not even Arthur.*

I reached for my Bible and turned to John's gospel. I found myself looking at the story of the woman of Samaria in chapter four, and the fourteenth verse stood out for me with new meaning: "Whosoever drinketh of the water that I shall give him shall never thirst; but the water that I shall give him shall be in him a well of water, springing up into everlasting life."

The spring of life. And Jesus had promised not only that it should be within me, but that rivers of living water should flow out of me. I wanted to shout and sing.

I walked to the supermarket, and I couldn't believe that the world outside was unchanged. The same tired faces of the people in the streets, the same crowded shops. When I paid for my goods at the till, I half expected the girl to ignore me as if I were invisible, or to stare at me as if she had seen a ghost. I walked and moved in the busy world as though I was not a real part of it. I felt detached, isolated, but aglow with a wordless joy.

For the next few days I had a heightened awareness of the tawdriness of life. Even the most innocuous television programs jarred on my spirit. The holiness of God touched everything I saw with a white light which threw everything else into shadow. I wanted to escape to a quiet, secret spot where no one could find me. I wanted to retreat. I felt in need of an Arabia.

Inevitably, the next thing that happened was that I began to try and analyze what had happened to me: to classify my experience. I supposed that this was what I had heard described so often as "The Baptism of the Holy Spirit," and I began to wonder if I would speak in tongues. I told the Lord that if he wanted to bestow this gift upon me, then I was ready to receive it. My heart was so full of praise and adoration, that I longed for a new language in which to express it. I prayed, I opened myself ready for such a gift, but no gift came. *So be it, Lord.*

On the third day after the experience, I knew I must tell Arthur. I dreaded doing this, because I was afraid of somehow impairing our close, deep, love relationship. What if he should try to rationalize, or to explain away what happened to me? I couldn't bear that, and I couldn't face opening myself to such a possibility. I prayed for an opportunity, for a solution to my dilemma.

It came while we were eating our Tuesday lunch. Arthur began to talk about someone he knew who had claimed to have had a "charismatic" experience. Before he could express his usual doubts about "this kind of thing," I cut him short.

"Arthur. It's no good. You will have to know. This has happened to me, too."

He paled. "You mean you've spoken in tongues?" His voice was gentle, for he could see the misgiving in my eyes.

"No, no, no—not *that!*" As I spoke, I recognized the complete irrelevance and unimportance of the tongues issue, and at the same time knew that it was this issue which lay at the back of many of Arthur's doubts.

"Then tell me, darling. What's happened?"

We left the table, and I went to sit on the settee, tucking my feet up under me.

"I'm not going to be able to explain. I don't know where to begin. You see, there aren't any words that are really suitable. They won't fit . . ." I broke off, confused.

"Just tell me. I shall understand."

And I knew that he would.

When I had finished, the tears were running down both our cheeks. Arthur came and sat beside me, and took me in his arms. Without a word, he held me against him and covered me with kisses.

The next few days have become a blurr in my memory, but I know that they were very, very precious ones. One or two scenes are sketched with clear, tender lines upon my mind for ever.

It is the first night after I have shared these things with Arthur. We lie in our double bed, close together as always, when all at once Arthur turns and reaches for me, not as a lover, but as a child who has awakened in a dark room.

"Hold me," he pleads, brokenly. "Please hold me and don't let me go."

There is a note of real urgency in his voice, and I hold

him as a mother holds a frightened child.

We are walking by a river lined with trees in glorious autumn dress. Gold and bronze leaves lie thick under our feet, and rustle dryly together on the branches over our heads. Ahead of us is a bend in the river where the green banks seem to meet and merge. A willow bends low, skimming the water; a boat comes sailing serenely behind us, the afternoon sun jewels the disturbed water with a thousand dancing gems of gold.

We are in deep conversation. I speak of private, hidden things, resentments and fears which God had been bringing to the surface of my mind. I speak of the way in which creativity sometimes tries to dominate one's life; we talk of my writing, his painting. We share the inner conflicts we have always felt about these things, since we first met; the way in which one seems to have resolved it, only to find, years later, that the conflict is still there. We discuss the deep, almost pathological need of the artist, and the guilt which comes with it when the artist is a Christian.

I go on to give voice to some of my complex feelings about the sexes. I tell how I see that I have allowed resentment to build up over the years against the stream of abuse which seems to me to come from literature, drama, serious plays and comedy whenever men talk about women. I ask him why this is. Why are men so contemptuous about women? I do not want to feel resentment, but I cannot understand why these things should be.

He stops on the towpath and looks into my eyes with a deep, tender love. He lifts his hand to my face and traces the outline of my cheeks and my mouth, gently, adoringly. Then he bends and kisses me with a lover's kiss.

We set out for a day in London. Usually when we do this, we separate at a given point and meet again later. Arthur loves to delve in second-hand bookshops and picture galleries; I prefer to walk, or browse around the big stores. But on this occasion, Arthur says:

"I can't explain it, but I feel I want you by my side. I don't want to see you walk away from me, even for a few hours. Shall we do something together?"

We decide to go to Hampstead Heath, take a picnic lunch and spend the day exploring the country stretches of the Heath together. Another day of precious closeness and communion. I see that our relationship, far from being in any way marred, is enriched and enhanced. How can anything of such a divine nature do anything other than beautify?

As the days go by, I begin to see my beautiful encounter in a shifting perspective. I begin a notebook, and the first entry in it reads like this:

> The dreadful joy thy Son has sent
> Is heavier than any care:
> We find, as Cain his punishment
> Our pardon more than we can bear."

Arthur reads this, and says: "I would never have dreamed you needed any purging."

I look at him and say: "Purging is not really the right word. Healing is nearer the mark."

I see that he does not understand; but I am only just beginning to understand myself.

5

ONE OF THE FIRST LESSONS I had to learn was that spiritual experience cannot be standardized. My attempts to classify my own particular experience of renewal soon taught me that the leaders of the charismatic movement often make one fundamental mistake. They assume that because one person reaches a crisis in his life which brings him to the point of a "second blessing," then any Christian who has not reached this point is "incomplete," does not know the Spirit's fulness. (And any minister who does not preach about "the baptism" does not preach the full gospel.) They produce scriptures to support all this, naturally.

It follows from this, according to their reasoning, that if one such "Spirit-filled" believer received the gift of tongues, then all should do so. The "gift" is then regarded as proof that the person has really been "baptized in the Spirit." Furthermore, they affirm, there are other gifts of the Spirit which are available to us all—gifts such as healing, prophecy and the power to cast out devils. The Spirit-filled Christian will often use his gift of tongues in public worship; he will sing in the spirit, he

will clap his hands, raise them to heaven in worship; he
may even get up and dance. He has been liberated from
all his inhibitions; there are now no holds barred. Everyone should know this liberty! What is more, if you cannot
enjoy such liberty, then there is something seriously
lacking in your spiritual experience.

But such is human nature that this kind of liberty is in
danger of turning into bondage. As soon as these Christians begin to point their fingers at other believers and
say: "You should be doing these things too," the very
spirit of liberty and love is broken. A sense of spiritual
superiority all too often creeps in, and this, taken to its
logical conclusion, may become authoritarian and legal-
istic. Under such leadership, a "liberated" people may
well find itself enmeshed in a different kind of bondage;
and for the sensitive, thinking person, confusion and
even mental breakdown may result.

I say this, not to belittle a movement which I believe
has been greatly used of God to bring spiritual renewal to
thousands of his people, but because I have witnessed
the harm that can be done when particular aspects of
biblical teaching are isolated and developed to an extreme: an extreme which I believe to be alien to the truth
of the gospel, and dishonoring to the name that is above
all other names.

When I saw that my own "divine encounter" would
not really fit the charismatic picture, I began to read
books which I felt might throw light on the matter. I
found that through the ages, many people had entered
into an experience of spiritual renewal such as mine—
people from all walks of life, from different religious
backgrounds and holding widely different viewpoints
about biblical interpretation. At first this frightened me. I
began to feel that I would rather not know about these

other people. It would be safer to remain in ignorance. But then I saw that, for the one who is honestly seeking the truth, there is nothing to fear. Was I not one with the very spirit of truth himself? Had he not promised to lead me into all truth?

I realized that so many well-meaning evangelicals have closed their minds to all but the clearly defined truths they have been taught since childhood. They have not done so deliberately in every case, but out of an inbred fear of departing from truth into error. And because they have grown accustomed to regarding all spiritual experience that does not fit comfortably under the evangelical umbrella as "unsound," they have, in fact, become content with embracing half-truths: they have put themselves into blinkers for their own comfort. Since they only read a certain type of book, they are not likely to have their complacency much disturbed. Since many of them rarely converse in any depth with unbelievers, or believers of other persuasions, their knowledge of total human and spiritual experience is minimal.

I found, in my search for a unifying element for the kind of encounters with the eternal which I shall loosely label mystical, that certain ingredients were common to practically all such experiences. These were a sense of utter worthlessness, and an abandoning of the selfhood to God, followed by an awareness of a consuming love, and an ecstatic joy that defies verbal expression.

F. C. Happold, philosopher, historian and scholar of some standing, who himself made such an investigation as mine but on a much wider scale, following an experience which changed his whole life, has summed it up like this:

"There are times when the awakened soul, craving for a revelation which will make sense of the riddle of the

universe, of the apparent futility of life, and of its own
inadequacy, may feel that there is no answer. Sick with
longing, it can only cry, *De profundis Domine*. But the
desire is everything; for the prayer of desire is not seldom
the prelude of the revelation. Suddenly the 'timeless
moment' is there, the morning stars sing together, a
sense of utter joy, utter certainty, and utter worthlessness mingle, and in awe and wonder it murmurs: *I
know*."

I recorded my findings in my notebook, and I did so
without fear, for the new sense of oneness with God
given to me when he revealed himself to me that morning, had left me with the awesome assurance that whatever I did with my right hand, my left hand was safely
enclosed in his—as the hand of a child might be enclosed
in the hand of its father—and that, provided I did not
draw my hand away, the whole of my being was in his
control.

To illustrate the diversity of the mystical experience, I
quote here from two sources—the first is from that well-
known American evangelist, D. L. Moody, and the second from F. C. Happold, the English scholar whose
pedigree I have just mentioned.

D. L. Moody writes: "I was crying all the time that God
would fill me with his Spirit. Well, one day in the city of
New York—oh, what a day!—I cannot describe it, I seldom refer to it: it is almost too sacred an experience to
name.... Paul had an experience of which he never
spoke for fourteen years ... I can only say that God
revealed himself to me, and I had such an experience of
his love that I had to ask him to stay his hand. I went
preaching again. The sermons were not different; I did
not present any new truths; and yet hundreds were
converted. I would not now be placed back where I was

before that blessed experience if you should give me all the world—it would be as the small dust of the balance."

F. C. Happold writes:

"It happened in my room in Peterhouse on the evening of 1st February, 1913, when I was an undergraduate at Cambridge. If I say that Christ came to me, I should be using conventional words which would carry no precise meaning; for Christ comes to men and women in different ways. When I tried to record the experience at the time, I used the imagery of the vision of the Holy Grail; it seemed to me like that. There was, however, no sensible vision. There was just the room with its shabby furniture, and the fire burning in the grate and the red-shaded lamp. But the room was filled with a presence, which in a strange way was both about me and within me, like light or warmth. I was overwhelmingly possessed by someone who was not myself, and yet I felt I was more myself than I had ever been before. I was filled with an intense happiness, and almost unbearable joy, such as I had never known before and have never known since. And over all was a deep sense of peace and security and certainty."

The total difference between the two men, their religious backgrounds, their education, their conditioning, and hence their differing modes of expression and style of writing, is obvious. But both experienced a divine encounter which changed their lives, and which, though they rarely spoke of, they would never be able to forget.

By way of definition, Happold writes:

"It is the way of union through reciprocal love, of like calling unto like, of the love of God stretching down to man and of the love of man stretching up to God. But it is not an easy way. It is the royal road of the holy cross, a way of utter self-loss, of the shedding of every vestige of self-love, of the abandonment of everything, even of one's own selfhood. But the supreme loss is the supreme finding. Within the wild desert of the naked godhead is found the divine bridegroom to whom the soul, all cares and shame forgotten, is united in the garden of lilies, the dear comrade, the heavenly Father with outstretched arms who is also the mother on whose breast the weary child may rest, the redeemer, and mediator, a love encompassing everything."

How dare we try to confine such a God to the narrow strait-jacket of our own limited vision, our own pre-conceived, stereotyped ideas? Or even try to match him up to our own particular interpretation of Scripture? How dare we mould him to a pattern of our own making, expecting him to conform to type as we so often do ourselves? He will not be typecast, he will not be regimented, he will have nothing to do with our small-minded attempts at uniformity. When on earth Jesus once said, speaking of his forthcoming death, "And how am I straitened until it be accomplished!" But when he had accomplished all things, he came as the wind, the fire—invisible, unpredictable, untamable just as he said he would. "The wind bloweth where it listeth: thou canst not tell whence it cometh or whither it goeth: so is everyone who is born of the Spirit."

When we try to classify or categorize our experience of God, we are trying to harness the wind. Nor can we explain or understand why he comes to some in one way, to others in a different way. Because one person is given a certain type of revelation, that does not make him in any way superior to the person who may never enter into that particular kind of experience. It goes without saying that I know myself to be a far less worthy person than many saints who have known nothing of a supernatural encounter. But as to reasons, they are not mine to give.

One thing is clear: on the road to God, none may bypass the cross of Christ, and the principle of dying to self in order to live is at the root of every genuine spiritual rebirth. A man may go through all the motions of an authentic evangelical type conversion, but unless he dies to self he remains unregenerate. "Except a corn of wheat fall into the ground and die, it remaineth alone." I believe there are many people both inside and outside the church today who are the victims of what has been called "easy-believism." Years ago, maybe, they went through the motions of a conversion experience, but today they are so much dead wood because they have never known real conviction of sin, never died to self. The New Testament warns against such counterfeit spiritual experience.

Similarly, a believer may go through all the motions of being baptized by the Holy Spirit. His friends may pray with and for him, hands may be laid on his head; he may be told that no matter whether he feels any different or not, if he has "asked the Holy Spirit to fill him" then he is filled; he may even find himself enveloped in feelings he cannot explain: but if there has not been a willingness to shed every vestige of self-love, then there will be no genuine spiritual renewal.

The spiritual Fathers of the East talked of a sin called spiritual greed which is really a thinly disguised lust for power. I believe we need to be closely on our guard against this sin. There is only one road to a closer union with God, and that is the way of the cross, the way of renunciation, the way of self-loss. And it is a rough and painful road.

Just how rough and how painful my own road was yet to be I could not guess in those first ecstatic days of joy and wonder. But the supreme loss is the supreme finding.

6

THREE YEARS HAD PASSED since Elizabeth left home to start her nursing training. Kissing her good-bye in the dingy nurses' home which was attached to the hospital, I felt that I was entrusting my one ewe lamb to an alien world. The matron had looked as if she were the worse for drink, the hospital itself looked Victorian and cheerless, and the room where Elizabeth was to make her home looked in need of a good Spring clean.

At home, I stood in her bedroom—bright and light and alive with color—and surveyed the two single beds with a heavy heart. My two chicks had flown the nest: Frankie to the celestial city, Elizabeth to a very different kind of city. For the first week I worried in case she should be homesick; for the second week I worried in case she shouldn't! At last she telephoned to say that all was well, and she was enjoying herself.

Elizabeth had always wanted to be a nurse. After Frankie's death, I half expected her to change her mind, having spent a good deal of time in hospital wards with us on visiting days, and having witnessed firsthand the ravages of disease and sickness. But when the time came, there was still no other idea than nursing in her mind, and when she left school she did a pre-nursing course at the local Tech.

But temperamentally she was not really suited to nursing. Although she stuck it out to the end of the course, it was to have a detrimental effect upon her health. Worse even than this was the effect those years were to have on her emotionally. The spiritual wilderness into which she passed was eventually to close in on her with painful results to us all.

Of all this we knew nothing at the time it was actually transpiring. She came home on regular visits, talked brightly and freely about her life in the hospital, and if occasionally she seemed depressed, it was no more than was to be expected of a young girl living such an entirely different kind of life from the one to which she had been accustomed, with all the pressures that caring for the sick and chronically ill can put upon anyone. If she spoke rarely of church activities, we simply attributed this to the fact that irregular off-duty hours made it difficult to be really involved with the life of any one church.

Just a year before she left home, she had been baptized, and had given a clear testimony to the presence of Christ in her life. I had been moved to tears that night when Arthur baptized her. As she stood at the front of the church in her white blouse and grey skirt, I thought how much like her Daddy she was in temperament—reserved, never ready to speak out what was in her heart; yet keenly sensitive to spiritual truth, and always on her guard against any kind of sham. I had felt that these qualities would stand her in good stead when the time came for her to leave home.

But there came a time when we knew that all was not well with Elizabeth. One Sunday evening when she was at home she came to church with us as usual, but just before the communion service was about to begin, she suddenly got up out of her seat and hurried out of the church. As soon as the service was over, I rushed home to see if she was all right. I found her standing by the fireplace leaning on the mantelpiece, her head bent.

"Are you all right? Why did you rush out like that?" I asked anxiously.

She made no answer, but, with a letter opener that had been lying on the tiled mantelpiece, she poked at the cement that held the tiles together. Sure now that something was wrong, I pressed her gently for an answer.

"I didn't think I should stay . . . I've neglected things," she said. Her voice, her posture, the tension in her body took me back to that day just before Frankie had died. In just such a manner as she now stood by the mantelpiece, she had then stood by the draining board in the kitchen of our Sussex Manse, pressing the handle of a spoon on to the hardness of the surface as she now pressed the ivory letter opener.

"But look dear," I reasoned, "if you feel you've let things slip a bit, surely a communion service is the place to put it right, get back into fellowship with God again?"

She went on picking at the tiles with the letter opener.

"It's no good, Mummy."

"What isn't any good?"

"I can't explain. . . ."

"But can't you just try? I expect I'd understand . . . we've always talked things over, haven't we?"

"It's no *good*, Mummy!" And she walked past me and went up to her room.

Arthur and I prayed for her every day. We felt so helpless, but knew that of ourselves there was nothing we could do—only keep ourselves open, as we had al-

ways tried to do, ready to listen and understand. Sometimes she would ring up, just for a chat, but she usually
ended up by saying how unhappy she was, and how, as
soon as she had sat her finals, she intended to get out of
nursing. But more of her heart than that, she seemed
unable to reveal.

She left nursing, and took a temporary job in a book-
shop, but stayed on in her London flat. Things seemed to
return to normal after that. Elizabeth stayed to communion whenever she was at home, and talked a bit about the
church she attended while away. The crisis, if crisis there
had been, seemed to have passed.

At about the time of the experience described in the
previous chapter, I began to feel my daughter being
placed very specially on my heart. I was learning new
lessons in prayer every day, finding out more about
intercession, and fellowship with the Father. One thing I
learned was that in praying for individuals, it was good
not to try to be too specific, but just to commit that one as
a whole person to God. This I did for Elizabeth, among
others, but with a special burden of mother-love behind
my prayers.

Then one day she rang to say that something had
happened that she knew we would want to hear about:
she had met up with an ex-boyfriend who was now at
university, and in talking to him had been made to feel
thoroughly ashamed of what had become of her Christian faith and witness. The ex-boyfriend had joined a
Christian union, had obviously grown spiritually, and
Elizabeth had wanted us to know that as a result of
talking with him, she had come back to the Lord.

We wept for joy. But as with all experiences of spiritual
renewal, it was only a beginning. We could not guess,
then, the pain that had yet to be endured before God's

surgery was complete. Elizabeth now moved into a flat with three other Christian girls. These girls had two things in common: they each had their problems, and they were each drawn toward the charismatic movement. For Elizabeth there came a complete spiritual renewal. It was another rebirth, but this time the travail was long and painful. When the Holy Spirit began his work of liberation in her heart, the purging and the healing were to strike with the ruthlessness of a surgeon's knife at the roots which had been growing furtively for years.

There came a day when Elizabeth began to pour out to us—in spurts, and in long spates, the hidden hurts and resentments which had festered in her mind over the years. It was an agonizing, and, of course, intensely personal time in all our lives, and I have only included certain parts of it here because of the relation it bears to my own spiritual journey. For there were points at which our experiences overlapped and there was a sense in which the purging and healing that came to Elizabeth were my purging and healing too. So complex and subtle are the threads that make up the fabric of our lives, so obscure and strong are the forces which bind humankind together, and so darkly sensitive is the mechanism of the human mind that I wonder afresh how anyone dares to embark on the journey of life, or to enter into any of life's human relationships, without faith in a Father-Creator.

Elizabeth began by telling us how, during the period of her sister's illness she had felt totally rejected—not necessarily by us, but by her whole world. She had felt herself to be surrounded by people who had no idea how she was feeling. This, she saw now, was partly due to the fact that she herself had been incapable of accepting the emotional trauma of the situation. She had, in order to cope with living, locked a door in her mind and thrown away the key. To herself and to others, she pretended she did not have a sister who was seriously ill. She lived and talked as though it were not happening. She was incapable of seeing, at the time, that her attitude produced puzzlement and unspoken hostility in those who were fully aware of the agony of our situation. She felt that the whole world was against her. She was rejected.

"Do you remember that weekend a few years back when Pauline and June came to stay?"she asked me. "How I got all your books off the shelf and hid them at the back of my cupboard?"

I nodded, remembering only too clearly the shock and hurt of finding them there when the girls had gone.

"It was because of *Beyond the Shadows*. I was afraid that seeing your storybooks might lead the girls to talk about *that*. You see, I even resented that you had written it—I wanted the whole thing forgotten, blotted out. I was angry with you for making it live on by writing a book about it."

I listened in stunned silence. After all the care we had taken, the conscious effort we had made all through to see that she was not left out, not neglected. I just could not believe it. Yet such is mother-love, such the complexity and the pain of it, that even while my mind protested against this attack on that tender, bruised area of my memory, I was aware of the nagging beginnings of doubt and guilt. Had I neglected her? Had I given her enough love? Had I been so wrapped up in the child who I knew must, before long, be snatched from my arms, that the one who was to be mine to love for many years to come had been left out in the cold? If so, then such inadequacy had been entirely unconscious. But unconscious or not, was I guilty? Had I failed as a mother? Had I lost one child and damaged another?

Memories crowded in. Frankie had been so easy to show love to. She had been affectionate, outgoing, demonstrative. If I touched her she would return the touch eagerly; if I put my arms around her, she wound hers around my neck and covered my face with kisses. She said "I love you" whenever it came into her mind. Not long before she had died, she wrote these three precious words on two pieces of paper and handed one to me, and the other to her Daddy. She was that kind of child.

But Elizabeth was temperamentally opposite. If I touched her she made little response. She did not invite embraces; her kisses, when she gave them, were stiff and shy. There was something in her personality that lacked spontaneity. She couldn't help it, any more than Frankie could help being spontaneous. She gave every outward sign of shrinking from expressions of affection. How then was I to know she longed for them, if long for them she did? But was I guilty, was I guilty? That was the thing I wanted to know.

"You know when you said to me, after Frankie had died, that you would be able to give me more of your time now?"

I nodded, bracing myself for another blow. It came. She said in a small voice:

I thought to myself, "Don't bother."

Please, Lord, no more. Don't let there be any more. But there was to be more.

I was doing some work in my bedroom, and Elizabeth came and sat down on the bed.

"Mummy, I want to tell you about the time when I was away from the Lord . . . about some things that happened while I was nursing. I should have told you before, but I didn't want to hurt you any more. But now I have to talk about it. The Lord has put it all right for me; he's healed it all. At least, he's still doing it, he's doing it now. And part of the healing has got to be sharing it with you."

She begins to tell me, tracing her path through the dark wilderness, sparing me nothing. I sit beside her on the bed and listen. As I listen, I feel that there is a point in the heart's suffering where pain becomes something else. It passes beyond pain into a kind of suspension of reality. I had felt it many times during Frankie's illness. I feel it now. When at last her story is finished, we turn to each other. I do not know who makes the first move, but suddenly we are in each other's arms, weeping and comforting. Only, now she is the chief comforter, I am the comforted. And it is in this that we find our salvation and our release. For a moment we are no longer mother and daughter, but two women crying in each other's arms. Her young body is soft and slender against mine. The unfamiliarity of her embrace, the strangeness of her touch, makes me realize that she is feeling the same about me. I put her back from me for a moment to ask:

"Was it my fault? Am I to blame?"

But now she starts to cry again, shaking her head, and reaching for me blindly.

"No, no, nobody's fault. Nobody's to blame—except me, of course. But then the Lord has dealt with all that. He's cleansed and healed me. It's all right now."

That night in bed, I tell Arthur all that Elizabeth has said to me. The floodgates burst, and I sob as if my heart would break. I dread that he will be as shattered as I am, but he is strong, strong and calm.

"If anyone is to be blamed," he says, "it's I. Didn't she say she couldn't talk to me? Didn't she say she resented me for the tension I caused in her? If anybody has failed as a parent, it's I."

But I shake my head and sob all the louder, clinging to him as though I am drowning in a stormy ocean. He holds me close and strokes my hair, and I blurt out:

"And I thought I was the strong one!"

He holds me closer, and after a while he whispers:

"The Lord knows it all."

Tozer says that self is the opaque veil that hides the face of God from us, and it can be removed only in spiritual experience, never by mere instruction. "Let us remember," he says, "that when we talk of rending the veil, we are speaking in a figure, and the thought of it is poetical, almost pleasant; but in actuality there is nothing pleasant about it. In human experience that veil is made of living spiritual tissue; it is composed of the sentient, quivering stuff of which our whole beings consist, and to touch it is to touch us where we feel pain. To tear it away is to injure us, to hurt us and make us bleed.... That is what the cross did to Jesus, and it is what the cross would do to every man to set him free. Let us beware of tinkering with our inner life in hope ourselves to rend the veil. God must do everything for us. Our part is to yield and trust."

But while the pain of the rending is at its height, it is hard to trust, hard to remember that he is perfect love.

7

JUST HOW LARGE a part the question of guilt, whether real or imagined, plays in the sicknesses of mankind, both physical and emotional, we shall perhaps never know. I have found in talking to women of every kind, that many are haunted by feelings of guilt about human relationships. "How much was I to blame in this or that thing?" they ask. "Had I behaved otherwise, said this, or not said that, would things have been different?" Some say, "I knew I should not be behaving like that, but I somehow wasn't able to help it." Others tell how they honestly believed that they always acted with love and care and sensitivity in their family situations—yet in spite of all their efforts, things have gone wrong.

Most men do not seem to suffer unduly from guilt feelings in this area—perhaps because the whole complex business of making relationships work is usually considered to be woman's province. It is, perhaps, her highest calling. And if she fails she suffers from deep feelings of inadequacy and guilt.

Sometimes guilt feelings are quite irrational, or apparently so. I remember that my first reaction when told that

Frankie was going to die was one of guilt. I felt I must have sinned in some way to bring such a thing to pass. Other mothers of sick children have told me the same thing. *Is it my fault?* they cry within themselves. *I must be somehow to blame.* One mother who lost a child said that she felt a terrible, irrational sense of guilt because she had not been able to keep her little one alive. Where do such feelings come from?

Guilt feelings about Frankie's death were among the first ones to come to the surface after the Lord had met with me that Saturday morning, and shown me his glory. It was as though, having first been enfolded in the arms of his love, I must next pass through the painful process of healing. I was to experience that love in its very fulness, provident and venerable as a father's love for a child; jealous, inexorable, exacting as love between the sexes. This kind of love spares us nothing.

I was faced once more with the whole question of my writing career. Had I put it before my children? Though I knew that I had not, the lurking doubt that I had given it too prominent a place in my life, that it had become too important to me, remained. Though I knew I had surrendered it to God that morning, given it back to him, counted it but worthless compared with the joy of knowing him fully, yet the years of conflict, the secret, nagging doubts, the probing sense of guilt, had left their marks. These were the wounds that had to be cauterized and healed.

I now came into the blessed realization, so often spoken of but never fully experienced until this time, that the death of Jesus on the cross was for this purpose. That his blood covered all my sins, conscious or unconscious, sins of omission as well as sins of commission. For I came to see afresh that sin, whether it be deliberately or un-

consciously committed, is still an offence against the
holiness of God, and must be dealt with before we can
know him in the sense that Jesus meant in John 17:3. The
Epistle of John became very precious to me. "If we walk
in the light, as he is in the light, we have fellowship one
with another, and the blood of Jesus Christ his Son
cleanseth us from all sin."

These words have become so meaningful to me that I
feel I want to give them afresh to every anxious, fretful
soul who is trying to unravel the complexity of her total
experience, or to cover it all up in a comfortable cloak of
pretence. I want to say, I have good news for you! There's
no need to worry anymore, no need to cover up the past
in your mind. God knows what helpless, bungling creatures we all are. He knows too that we are often as much
sinned against as sinning; that we are often victims of our
parents' shortcomings, as they in turn have been victims
of heredity, or of the sins of their forbears.

Bruised or damaged by their inadequacies, we are yet
compelled, by the very nature of things, to go on bruis-
ing or damaging our own offspring. Don't be afraid to
admit your own guilt, your own part in the human
condition. John said that if we say we have no sin, we lie,
and the truth is not in us. Does it not follow then, that we
are bound to sin—we are inheritors of our first parents'
fallen nature. The only unpardonable sin is to pretend to
ourselves and to God we have no sin. For how shall we
taste of the remedy if we will not admit to the malady?

When John wrote, "We have fellowship one with
another," he referred primarily to the fellowship between God and his child. *God and you.* ("For surely our
fellowship is with the Father," he wrote.) Such a precious union is made possible only through Jesus Christ.
It is his blood that cleanses us from sin, restoring us to

fellowship with the Father, making us one with him for ever.

No wonder Paul said he counted all things but loss that he might know him. For to know him is life eternal. Yet we return once more to the old familiar principle: the water in that spring of life cannot be dispensed to us freely until we have surrendered our jugful of proud resistance. And even this act of surrender is not of our doing. It is the work of the Holy Spirit. If we do not know the fulness of God's love, the free outpouring of his Spirit, it is because we are afraid to walk in the light. We would rather keep certain things hidden. We must at all costs preserve our self-esteem. But it is when we let go that we shall possess; when we lose our life that we shall find it; with each death to self comes new supplies of life.

We must "die daily" in order to "keep on being filled with the Spirit." We are wrong if we think that the Holy Spirit comes to us once for all, in his fulness, either at conversion or at a time of second blessing. In a sense, there is a once-for-all element in it, because he does come to take up his abode in us at the time of our initial surrender to him; but thereafter we must continually draw water from the well of salvation. He does not dispense his blessing to us automatically, any more than the pump in the meadow on my father's farm gave water without being primed and then pumped. The priming in our lives must be a daily surrender to his will. Otherwise, step by subtle step we shall cause the spring of life to run dry in us.

Behind many of the modern religious ideas which have been so helpful to thousands in recent years, this principle lies, though at times heavily disguised. The books on praise which took the evangelical world by storm in recent years—in spite of their off-center suggestion that God is directly responsible for everything that befalls us, including the sins of others—did good wherever they were interpreted as saying that God is sovereign in the life of the believer. In other words, if we surrender to his will in everything, letting go of our own self-interest, no matter how hurtful that may be to us at the time, then blessing must follow.

I proved this myself over what will undoubtedly seem to others quite a minor matter. It was not, however, minor to me—and are not our lives made up of such seemingly trivial happenings? I had promised to go and address a meeting some distance from my home town on the subject of "Christian Joy." Just as I was setting out on the journey, the postman brought me a letter which knocked all the joy out of my heart with a single blow. The letter did not contain bad news as such, but it did contain some unjust and bitter words from someone whom I had gone out of my way to help. I was deeply hurt. The lovely sunny day was spoiled; the prospect of the long train journey, which I normally enjoy, lost its appeal; the thought of standing up in front of two hundred women and speaking on Christian joy suddenly became impossible. So bad did I feel that I actually reached for a set of notes for a previous talk I had given on another subject to take with me on the journey, in case the "Joy" talk should completely die on me.

On the journey I did my best to forget the letter. I told myself that the writer was sick, and therefore not really answerable for her uncharitableness. I prayed that the Lord would take away my feeling of depression. But the depression remained.

I looked at my notes. And then I realized that I had planned to speak of the possibility of knowing joy at all times—even when things were going wrong. I was going to tell these women how I found it possible to experience joy during my daughter's illness. Yet I had not learned how to feel joy at a time of personal attack because of a mere matter of hurt pride. I knew that this hurt must be surrendered to God just as much as the big hurt of grief and suffering—that at root it was self-pity which was robbing me of joy. And I realized in that moment that it is sometimes easier to feel a supernatural joy, a special kind of God-given joy, in the dramatic crises of our lives, than it is to remain serene through the little irritations that come to all of us—and especially when someone has hurt our pride.

I surrendered my hurt to God in that moment—and as I had a carriage to myself on the train, I decided to follow the example of Paul and Silas, who, with sore backs and their feet in the stocks, had sung songs of praise to God in the middle of the night. The song I sang was a verse from Habakkuk!

> Yet will I rejoice in the Lord,
> I will joy in the God of my salvation:
> God the Lord is my strength!

I shared that experience with the women to whom I spoke later that afternoon. Quite unknown to me, the Holy Spirit was working in the hearts of at least two women in that church, and both of them wrote to tell me later how their lives had been changed as a result of that message.

The first was a young wife who had come to the meeting almost by chance, and had heard for the first time how God has "freely given us all things" with the gift of his Son to be our Savior. The second person was the minister's wife, who following the meeting, came into an experience of spiritual renewal very similar to my own.

Having written to tell me of it, she telephoned a year later, on the anniversary of the meeting, to tell me that that particular date would always be precious to her, and that she was still rejoicing in all that God had done for her since that day. Not only was her own life transformed but, through her ministry among the women of the church, the blessing was spreading out to others. The girl who had been converted had gone back to her own local church and started a house group in her home for Bible study, prayer and outreach. When next I heard from her, her husband was beginning to show a definite interest in spiritual things. Now he, too, has found Christ.

We never know what rivers of living water we are letting loose when we surrender our wills to him in every detail of our lives, when we rejoice in him even when it hurts us to do so and all around us seems to belie that joy. The secret lies, not in any power there might be in our praise, but in the surrender of our puny wills to his loving sovereignty.

8

IN C. S. LEWIS' children's story, *The Silver Chair,* Aslan the lion sends Jill out upon her spiritual journey with these words:

"Here on the mountain I have spoken to you clearly: I will not often do so down in Narnia. Here, on the mountain, the air is clear and your mind is clear; as you drop down into Narnia, the air will thicken. Take great care that it does not confuse your mind. And the signs which you have learned here will not look at all as you expect them to look, when you meet them there. That is why it is so important to know them by heart and pay no attention to appearances. Remember the signs, and believe the signs. Nothing else matters."

Remember the signs. But what are the signs? For the Christian pilgrim, they are summed up in one emblem—the cross. One sign, and yet it is a twofold sign, for the outstretched arms speak of love, while the upright pole points upward to heaven and downwards to earth, and speaks of self-giving.

> *The shape of love*
> *Is the shape of a cross*
> *For love is self-giving*

187

So begins one of my own poems in my book *The Innermost Room*. The book was written before the experience of renewal described in the previous chapters, and sometimes when I look at its pages, I ask myself, "How did I know that *then*?" How could I have written those words before I had really lived them out fully in my own experience? Can one know a truth before it has become part of one's experience? In a sense, of course, we can; but, as someone has said, the truth we know is dangerous to us unless we live it.

In the pages of this book, I have compelled myself to take a look at the totality of my experience of God, and I have seen in doing so that there is a certain timelessness about God's dealings with us. He is not nearly so concerned about chronology as we are. One day to him is as a thousand years. He knows the end from the beginning This was one of the very first things that Arthur said to me when we began our courtship twenty-seven years ago.

Sometimes when I look back over my life, the events and emotions of the years seem to blur into one another to form a design which is totally abstract. Viewing my experience as a painting—as yet only partially completed—certain motifs seem to repeat themselves, almost at random, so that their actual placing in the sequence of events becomes irrelevant, their significance lies in what they contribute to the whole.

The tears my mother wept when she felt her daughter had become a stranger to her become the tears I wept over Elizabeth's wilderness wanderings. My father's voice raised in uncontrolled anger over some trivial thing becomes my own voice raised in anger when my own children quarreled. The terror in my infant heart becomes the fear in the eyes of my own little girls as they cringe from the heat of my anger. Arthur's fingers tracing the outline of my face as we walk by the river after my divine encounter, become Frankie's childish fingers hungrily stroking my face as she lay in the hospital bed. *"Don't go, don't go. I love you so much."* Her arms reaching for me the night before she dies become Arthur's arms reaching for me on that other night in the darkness of our bedroom. Her *"Cuddle me"* becomes his *"Hold me."* Voices, kisses, lips and hands and reaching arms, these are the recurring motifs I see, but the color in which they are painted is one color. The color of love.

I see my father putting up a swing for us in the apple tree, or taking the trouble to procure for us an old baker's van, and setting it against the back of the woodshed so that we might make it into a "little house," a hidey-hole; I see the pleasure in his eyes when he brings us presents back from market. . . .

Love lay behind the anger in my father's voice, the bitterness of my mother's tears. Love lay behind my own exasperation at my children's bickering, just as much as it lay behind everything else I did and was for them. Love lay behind the pleading hands and the pain-filled eyes, the hungry lips and the outstretched arms. And love lies behind every kind of reconciliation.

The two "I love you" notes that Frankie wrote for Arthur and me a few weeks before her death took exactly tens years to form an echo in her sister's words to us, but when the echo finally reverberated in our ears, its tone was doubly sweet. She came into the kitchen where the two of us were washing the dishes together, and spoke the words shyly but firmly, once to her father, with her arms about his neck:

"I love you, Daddy."

And next to me, embracing me from behind as I stood

at the sink.

"I love you, Mummy."

Her healing was almost complete, and so was ours.

C. S. Lewis, in his book *The Four Loves*, says that when we see the face of God, we shall realize that we have always known it, because he has been in all our earthly experiences of love. It will be like turning from the portraits of love to their original, from the rivulets to the fountain, from the creatures he made loveable to love himself. We shall, however, find them all in him, and by loving him more than them, we shall find that we love them even more than we did on earth.

When we remind ourselves that eternal life is knowing this God of love in a deep and intimate way, then we have no difficulty in accepting that this life eternal starts here and now; the minute we believe, we received it—we start out on the glorious adventure of knowing God through Jesus Christ whom he has sent. This knowing God is the very essence of the spring of life, which we may taste now, daily, but in whose waters we shall one day be totally and gloriously immersed.

Many Christians go through life trying to love an ideal, when God wants us to experience him as a loving personality. It was Jesus who showed to us the Fatherhood of God, and taught us to address him: "Our Father which art in heaven. . . ." "Behold, what manner of love," said John, "what love as from another country, the Father has bestowed upon us that we might be called the children of God!"

This unearthly love, which has in it both the love of a Father and of a lover, is available to every believer. We may not need to experience such love in a mystic fashion, or to regard it with the eyes of the visionary or the prophet, but we all need to experience it in our daily lives. If we do not know him in an intimate love relationship, then it is because we need to make a new surrender to his love, just as a wife surrenders to her husband's love before she can enjoy him fully.

Tozer says that when the eyes of the soul, looking out, meet the eyes of God looking in, heaven has begun right here on earth, and he goes on to quote from the sixteenth century saint, Nicholas of Cusa:

"When all my endeavour is turned toward thee, because all thy endeavour is turned toward me; when I look unto thee alone with all my attention, nor ever turn aside the eyes of my mind, because thou dost enfold me with thy constant regard; when I direct my love toward thee alone because thou, who art love's self has turned toward me alone. And what, Lord, is my life, save that embrace wherein thy delightsome sweetness doth so lovingly enfold me?"

What indeed? The one overwhelming revelation which I brought with me from out of my secret closet on that Saturday morning three years ago was that of being enfolded in an eternal embrace. This "delightsome sweetness" flavors everything I taste, colors everything I see, transforms every deed I do. Life is fuller, richer, more joyous than it ever was before. Instead of imposing restrictions, he has brought me into new liberations. Instead of narrowing my horizons, he has widened them. I look with fresh eyes upon all things lovely, all things true, all things of good report.

The whole earth is full of his glory. And, I think, if earth is so lovely, what must heaven be like? If creation is so glorious, what must its creator be like? If his embrace is so sweet now, what will it be like when our love is truly consummated? What will it be like to look on his face, to awake with his likeness?

And if at times now my heart nearly bursts with love for him, and praise of him, what will it be like when all my days are taken up with praise and adoration, when I am part of that heavenly host which ceaselessly adores him? For though I shall be but one of the host, yet I shall hold in my hand the white stone upon which will be written "a new name which no man knoweth saving he that receiveth it." That name will be compounded of all that the Lord has wrought in me; It will be the sum total of my experience of him; it will be the name he intended for me before the worlds began, a name which even in eternity will remain a secret between God and me.

In my beginning is my end.... And so I end as I began:

"Life eternal is nought other than that blessed regard wherewith thou never ceasest to behold me: Yea, even the secret places of my soul. With thee, to behold is to give life; 'tis unceasingly to impart sweetest love of thee; 'tis to inflame me to love of thee by love's imparting, and to feed me by inflaming, and by feeding to kindle my yearning, and by kindling to make me drink of the dew of gladness, and by drinking to infuse in me a fountain of life, and by infusing to make it increase and endure."

And this is life eternal, that I might know him, the only true God, and Jesus Christ whom he has sent. For he is the altogether lovely one, the source of all joy, the spring of life. It is for him, the living God, that the human heart is ever reaching.